witch school

Ritual,
Theory &
Practice

Photo © Debbe Tompkins

• • • •

About the Author

Rev. Donald Lewis-Highcorrell (Illinois) is the CEO of Witch School International, the largest online school of Witchcraft and Wicca. He is also the long-seated First Priest and Chancellor of the Correllian Nativist Tradition and principal author of the tradition's degree materials. Rev. Lewis-Highcorrell cofounded the Pagan Interfaith Embassy, where he serves as a Pagan Interfaith Ambassador to the United States. He is currently the studio head of Magick TV and producer and host of *Living the Wiccan Life*.

The Correllium, above, is the symbol of the Highcorrell family and the Correllian Tradition as a whole. The Correllium represents the oneness of being and is usually explained in this way: at the top, the Vault of Heaven is represented by (usually) a double line representing the elements of air and fire (light). At the center, a cross represents the element of earth and the four directions. At the bottom, a wave represents the element of water. The circle encompassing all is Spirit. The Correllium has its origin as a personal vision symbol and was later used in the manner of a familial crest.

Rev. Donald Lewis-Highcorrell

witch school

Ritual,
Theory &
Practice

Llewellyn Publications
Woodbury, Minnesota

First Printing, 2008
SECOND EDITION
(First edition © 2005 Witchschool.com)

Book design by Rebecca Zins
Cover design by Kevin R. Brown

Lewis-Highcorrell, Donald.
  Witch school ritual, theory & practice / Donald
Lewis-Highcorrell. — 2nd ed.
     p.   cm.
  ISBN 978-0-7387-1339-7
  1. Wicca. I. Title.
  BP605.W53L4925 2008
  299'.94—dc22

                    2008004161

Llewellyn Publications
A Division of Llewellyn Worldwide, Ltd.
2143 Wooddale Drive,
Dept. 978-0-7387-1339-7
Woodbury, MN 55125-2989
www.llewellyn.com

Printed in the United States of America

• • • •

Other Books by
Rev. Donald Lewis-Highcorrell

Witch School First Degree

Witch School Second Degree

Witch School Third Degree

To my brother Ed

Contents

Foreword

Greetings.

It has been my pleasure to prepare this course on ritual in theory and practice, in the hope of acquainting my readers with what I regard as the basic skills of group ritual leadership.

This course was originally prepared as a component in our larger Second Degree studies, and it is still a requirement for Second Degree. However, in its present form this book is made available to everyone, and with that comes a few points that must be made regarding the content of this course.

Because the original audience for this work was composed of people who had already passed our First Degree course, most of whom are First Degree Priesthood studying for Second Degree standing, there is no attempt made here to explain many features of ritual practice, as it is assumed that First Degree Priesthood will be familiar with these already.

Skills such as basic energy work, visualization, and divination—which are extremely important to the proper execution of ritual—are not taught in this volume, and instead are merely described in terms of how they are to be used in a given ritual. The same is also true for the nature, creation, and use of ritual tools. It is assumed that the reader already understands these things, and has built these various skills using the exercises and techniques taught in our First Degree coursework.

If in using this book you find that you need additional instruction in these areas, or if you simply wish to review what you already know, I strongly recommend our First Degree materials, which approach these issues from the ground up, so to speak.

Another issue that I should perhaps address is how to assign the parts in these rituals. In writing these materials I have often been intentionally vague about who is meant to enact specific parts of ritual, on the understanding that those studying come from many different circumstances.

Because this book was written as part of our Second Degree coursework, it was my assumption that I was speaking to prospective Second Degree Clergy who were in the process of learning to lead group ritual. Knowing how to lead group ritual is an important skill for the Second Degree Priest/Priestess, even if their personal vocation is solitary. The basics of solitary ritual are covered in our First Degree material and can be augmented by dozens of excellent books on the subject. Group ritual, however, is a different dynamic from solitary ritual, and the former is largely the dynamic this course is meant to address.

Nonetheless, I wrote the materials with the intention that the student should be able to adapt them to their personal needs. Thus it is assumed that a solitary practitioner will end up taking all parts in any given ritual, while a group will share the parts out according to their numbers. Even when roles of "Priestess" and "Priest" are referred to, the solitary practitioner must by necessity enact both. The same is true for the quarter calls, which may or may not be enacted by separate people, as well as the various rituals in which the quarters are personified. A solitary practitioner can take all four roles with ease, while a group will determine its actions by its numbers: the four quarter parts can be enacted by a single person, by two people each taking two quarters, or by a full complement of four people. It can even be expanded to eight people in some of these rituals, with four giving the quarter calls and four more personifying the quarters in rituals calling for such personification.

I wanted to be able to assure maximum flexibility in the materials so that they could be adapted with relative ease to the many different circumstances I knew my readers might be in. This does, however, in some cases make it difficult to tell exactly who is supposed to be doing what—because *you* the reader are meant to assign the parts, according to who you have available.

A final comment: this book is not about high magical ritual for personal growth and development. That sort of ritual is addressed directly in our main Degree materials, where it is usually presented more in the form of "pathworking" or visualization rather than as ritual per se. Personal development is extremely important to the Witch, but it is not the primary focus of this particular book. Instead, this book is about group ritual and community development through shared worship. Certainly the rituals given will aid in all participants' growth and development, but they also carry an important social purpose as well as their obvious spiritual purpose. This book is about ritual in the trenches, so to speak—a book for the person who is, or intends to be, leading a group, Shrine, or Temple, and who needs to be able to effectively coordinate group worship.

I hope that you enjoy this volume, and that you find it of use to you in your vocation.

May you Blessed Be,

Rev. Don

Rev. Donald Lewis-Highcorrell
FIRST PRIEST AND CHANCELLOR,
CORRELLIAN NATIVIST TRADITION

Chapter

I

Ritual Theory

In setting forth this section on ritual, it is not our intention to give you a book of immutable rituals to learn by rote and to practice without variation. Quite the contrary—ritual, like religion itself, is a living, growing thing. It adapts and changes according to the needs of those using it. The wise, whenever they find a better way, adapt it to their own. In doing so, we sacrifice none of our own traditions, but rather we help our traditions to grow and to improve.

The rituals in this section should be viewed as examples and templates, then: a starting place from which to gain facility with ritual and thence to create your own. For the art of ritual lies in mindful creating, not in mindless repeating.

The last thing the world needs is another "cookbook" of basic Wiccan rituals. There are so many of these already that one could fill a library with them alone. In putting this section together, we do offer a selection of rituals for you to draw upon, but we also hope to share with you the theory behind ritual as well as helpful tips learned from long years of performing ritual.

The rituals we will present are primarily oriented toward group or temple use but can also be used by the solitary practitioner. Generally speaking, the difference between group and solitary use is that solitary ritual tends to be simpler but more highly personal, since the ritualist can make use of symbols and concepts that have deep personal meaning without having to consider whether or not other people will understand them. For example, a solitary ritual can incorporate symbols from personal dreams or visions, which in a group ritual might not be appropriate or would require explanation.

. . . .
Ritual

Ritual should be an expression of the heart, whether the individual or the community heart.

Words, forms, actions—these serve only to help give form to the heart's expression and should never bind it. Granted, specific forms are sometimes important to give cohesion to group ritual or to pass along traditions that are important to the community. But in ordinary ritual, specific forms are a guideline from which the ritualist builds a personal expression.

There is no mistake greater than putting the form of a ritual above its function. Your concern in ritual must be that the ceremony achieves its purpose, not whether or not it uses specific words, movements, and so on.

Ritual serves three primary purposes:

First, ritual is an expression of religious devotion.

Second, ritual is a means of raising, directing, or attuning energy.

And third, ritual serves to create a sense of community with others, through common actions and through shared customs and traditions.

. . . .
Performance of Ritual

A ritual should never be "read," as from a script. With few exceptions, this creates a stilted, unnatural feeling. Using a script makes it very hard to raise energy, as people are apt to pay more attention to what they are reading than to what they are doing. It also tends to give the impression that the ritualist is an amateur who hasn't done this before and doesn't really know what they are doing.

Rather, the words and actions used in ritual should be your own; even the parts that are memorized should be put in a form that is natural and comfortable to you. This you develop through practice. Do not be afraid to rephrase, to innovate, and above all to improvise. In this way you make the ritual your own, and you will find that you are able to put more of yourself into it, thus raising more energy as well as being a purer expression of the ritual's intent.

People tend to be tense and nervous when they try to conform to the written words of others. There's also the possibility of messing up or losing one's place. Doing so can be embarrassing, and it can completely throw off the emotional and energetic feel of the ritual. When you use your own words you may still be nervous, but you are less likely to have problems.

Consequently, you should never carry a "script" into ritual. Familiarize yourself with the concepts and actions used in the given ritual, and then let your words flow naturally. Granted, you may wish to use a "script" the first couple of times you do a ritual, but if you must do this you should wean yourself from it as quickly as possible.

Instead of using a book or a script, you should write up an Order of Service for the ritual. This is a basic outline of the steps used in the ritual, which can be placed upon the altar and referred to during the ceremony. In some cases you might wish to give a copy of the Order of Service to each participant in the ritual, so that they know in advance what to expect and where they may be called upon to join in.

In addition, you might wish to have parts of the ritual written on note cards. This is especially useful for a ritual that deals with themes unfamiliar to some of the participants, such as beginning students or guests. You may also wish to use note cards during those few rituals—initiations, rites of passage, and so on—in which specific wording may be important because of custom or tradition. In all such cases, the use of note cards should be kept to a minimum as much as possible.

• • • •

Order of Service

Generally speaking, most rituals follow a very similar Order of Service. For that reason, most parts of the Order of Service become second nature as one gains more practice with ritual. Once the basic Order of Service has become second nature, it can be varied to fit the situation as needed or desired.

In the example given below, we use the formal circle casting preferred by the Correll Mother Temple, which you learned in the First Degree lessons. We prefer this circle casting for formal Correllian rituals like initiations. However, there are many ways to cast a circle, and in ordinary ceremonies you should not feel limited to this one. You should judge by your circumstances what is best for you and adapt accordingly. In later sections of this course we will introduce you to several other ways of casting the circle, but we will start with the formal Correllian casting.

This Order of Service is appropriate for the vast majority of rituals you will do. Because of this, the basic form will become second nature after you have done a few rituals. You should remember this material from the First Degree lessons, but you may wish to look back to the First Degree lessons in order to refresh your memory about the appropriate visualizations and suggested wording to use.

The Order of Service is divided into segments that correspond to the elements:

Air
- Clear and release all excess energy
- Bless the salt and the water
- Cleanse the ritual space, going tuathail and aspersing with the combined salt and water
- Bless the fire and air (usually incense)
- Charge the ritual space, going deosil and censing with the combined fire and air
- Cast the circle

Fire
- Call each quarter
  - Cleanse the quarter with salt and water
  - Charge the quarter with fire and air
  - Invoke the quarter
- Invoke the Goddess and God in a manner appropriate to the ritual
- Invoke the ancestors, if desired

Spirit
- Define and explain the focus and intent of the ritual
- The body of the individual ritual (act of power)

Water
- Bless the chalice (and "cakes" if desired)
- Share the chalice around the circle
- Offer what remains to the God/Goddess and the ancestors

Earth
- Thank the ancestors (if called)
- Thank the Goddess and God
- Thank and devoke each quarter
- Open the circle
- Cleanse and release all excess energy

The Order of Service should be kept on the altar in a discreet position, so that you can refer to it during the ceremony if you need to.

As stated, ritual should not be "read." There are exceptions to this, however. If you are working with people who do not have experience with ritual, you can make up note cards to assist them in taking a role in the ceremony, but this should be regarded as a temporary practice and you should soon wean yourself off of it. Also, some rituals have "mystery plays" in which a person will personify a deity. Not everyone has enough knowledge of theology to simply do this off the cuff, and note cards can again provide a solution. But, ideally, people should work to move past a reliance on note cards.

It is always best to prepare for a given ritual well in advance, so that you have time to familiarize yourself with its requirements. Think about how you will handle the ritual, and make yourself thoroughly familiar with its components. Commit to memory any part of the ritual you feel you should memorize, and try to have the Order of Service in your head as well as on the altar.

If it should come to pass that you make a mistake, even a big one, it is best not to call attention to it. Better to continue as if nothing had happened and correct the mistake without emphasizing it. If this can't be done, let it go altogether. As a rule, people will not notice. Even if they do notice, it will still be less disruptive than calling attention to the situation.

Of course, sometimes you may make a mistake that can be neither glossed over nor ignored. In that case, you should correct the matter in as considerate and dignified a manner as possible, apologize without being self-deprecating, and explain that mistakes are an ordinary, human part of ritual. Do not become flustered or overcompensate. Remember, you want people to be comfortable and to enjoy the ritual, not to feel embarrassed or awkward.

In writing this course, I have assumed I was writing for situations in which more than one person would be present. The rituals can for the most part be adapted to solitary use if desired, or expanded for group use by dividing the parts among as many people as are present.

In dealing with group ritual, problems present themselves that are not readily apparent in solitary ritual and are rarely touched upon in books on the subject. The first is boredom. Ritual works by raising and directing energy through thought and emotion. Lose these and you lose the energy. It is important in ritual to keep people interested and excited, and not to lose their attention. Alas, losing their attention is all too easy to do, and to a large extent you can only learn to avoid it through experience and by learning to recognize people's moods and expressions.

Yet some mistakes of this nature can be avoided easily. You will lose people's attention if you talk too long at any one time. You will lose their attention if you carry a meditation on too long. You will lose their attention if you go from person to person around a circle (as in a healing circle) too many times, and you will lose their attention if you have so many people in a circle that even going around once is tedious (as it would be when passing out the drink for the toast in a circle of forty or more people). In this last event you can avoid the problem by having more than one person serving, or by introducing a chant or other activity in the meantime. Having people waiting too long at any point is death to the energy of a ritual.

In any ritual, be careful with fire. If you are using a censer, cauldron, or burning dish, make sure it is suitable to the purpose. There is no such thing as being over-cautious. If you are not sure that you can do something safely, then don't do it.

Consider the needs of other people. If there are people in attendance who are allergic or otherwise unable to tolerate incense, don't use incense. Many incense alternatives have been enumerated in other places in our lessons. If there are people present who need to avoid alcohol, make sure you don't use wine in the chalice; use fruit juice or water instead. Be polite and make sure everyone else is, too.

Perhaps most importantly, don't forget to enjoy yourself. Ritual is meant to be a joyful, loving experience; allow it to be thus. Don't get caught up in the details,

and allow the experience to unfold as it needs to. Doing ritual should make you feel good; it should leave you feeling energized and strongly connected to the Divine. This is more important than any of the details.

In these pages I have attempted to treat ritual as a systematized pattern of interchangeable parts in order to emphasize a basic, simple order that can be expanded and re-dressed in any number of ways. If I have succeeded in my intention, upon completion of the course you will have the building blocks of an infinitely variable system of ritual form. You will also have many discrete examples of the component building blocks, which can be expanded still further by personal research.

All of this means nothing, however, if you do not put your heart into it. Ritual in the end is only a skeleton upon which emotion and faith put flesh. Too often people forget this, and are left with only the bare bones.

Chapter
II

New Moon Esbats

Esbats, as you will recall from the First Degree lessons, are the monthly rituals celebrated by Wiccans in time with the phases of the moon.

In our examination of ritual, we will begin with the Esbats. Most temples celebrate Esbats for the new moon and for the full moon, although some choose one or the other and a few celebrate only Sabbats.

To understand the purpose of the Esbats you must understand the lunar phases.

The moon represents the Goddess and also the soul, which has its origins in the Goddess. The moon represents our emotions and inner self, as well as the psychic and spiritual energies associated with the Higher Self. Consequently, it is believed that our psychic and magical abilities are affected by the phases of the moon, being strengthened as the moon waxes and grows full and turning inward when the moon wanes.

The new moon begins the moon's waxing phase, when she grows stronger and brighter, beginning as a slender crescent and building up toward full. This is the phase of the Maiden Goddess and the time for new beginnings and growth. At new moon we work for that which we wish to start and that which we wish to develop, either over the course of the month or over a longer term. It is a time to work on qualities we wish to cultivate, skills we wish to learn, behaviors we wish to perfect, and to focus on our goals.

The full moon is when the light of the moon is at its height in the middle of the cycle. This is the phase of the Mother Goddess. The full moon is generally considered to last for three days, one day to either side of the calendar date. This is when the energy of the moon is at its strongest, so it is a time to take advantage of the extra energy and to work on those things we most wish to manifest, since at full moon the lunar energies are pulling with us.

The waning moon is when the moon decreases from full back to a crescent and finally disappears. This is the phase of the Crone Goddess. During the waning moon we work on that which we wish to release, to cleanse, and to let go of. It is the time for endings. The waning moon is the time for internal growth and integration, just as the waxing moon is the time for external growth and development.

In ritual, we attune ourselves to these energies and work with them toward our personal goals.

. . . .

Ritual Considerations

The new moon is ruled by the Maiden Goddess. You may choose to invoke her as an archetype, or you may choose a specific form of the Maiden Goddess to invoke. You might choose a form of the Maiden that has personal significance to you or to the group, or you might select a form of the Maiden Goddess that has significance to the time of year or the astrological placement of the moon. For example, if the new moon is in Aries, you might choose the warrior Maiden Athena. If the new moon is in Taurus, you might consider a Goddess with bovine associations such as Hat-Hor or Lakshmi. Since the new moon occurs when the moon is in conjunction with the sun, the astrological placement of the new moon will be the same as that of the sun, although if you celebrate your new moon Esbat the night after the exact new moon, the moon may have moved on to a new sign.

Because the moons are lunar celebrations, some people invoke only the Goddess. Others like to invoke the God as well, for balance. For a new moon you would choose a God from the hero archetype, whose qualities are in sympathy with the Goddess being invoked.

Again, it is not necessary to choose a personal form of Deity to invoke; it is perfectly all right to invoke through archetype. This is up to you.

The second major consideration in setting up your ritual is an *act of power*. The act of power is a spell, visualization, or divination intended to use the energies of the ritual either to help the individuals present in some way or to give them information. Every ritual should include an act of power. Below I include several examples of acts of power that you might use at a new moon, but these are merely suggested possibilities.

It is also good to select several appropriate chants to use during the ritual, as people enjoy chants and they help to raise energy. If space permits, simple dances also help to raise energy, even just dancing in a circle. Remember, as we discussed in the First Degree lessons, sound affects the vibration of energy. This is one reason why chants are useful in circle. Chanting is not only enjoyable, but it also has a real effect on the magical energies being raised.

The ritual below is written as if for a woman and a man. This is merely for convenience. It can just as easily be performed by a single person, by simply treating the two parts as one. The gender of the ritualist is not important. The ritual can be adapted to a larger group by dividing each part between several people.

Having considered these things, let us move on to the subject of this section: a new moon Esbat.

. . . .

Air

What follows is the portion of the ritual that is identified with air: the cleansing of the ritual space and casting of the circle. The form we are using here might be considered a formal Correllian casting—that is, the form of casting that would be most commonly encountered in formal Correllian rituals at the Tradition level. That does not mean it is the only kind of circle casting used, or that it is the most common form used in ordinary ritual. In practice, there are many ways to cast a circle and in subsequent lessons we will illustrate several.

Begin by clearing and releasing all excess energy as usual. Release all tensions and anxieties. Just let them flow through and out of your body, like a gentle wave of energy, exiting through the soles of your feet.

The priestess cleanses the salt, making three tuathail circles above it with her hand, while visualizing yellow-white light. She imagines the light forcing out all negative or unfocused energy from the salt. The priestess speaks words to the effect of:

Priestess: *"Behold, I exorcise you, O creature of earth, casting out from you any impurities that may lie within."*

Then the priestess blesses the salt, making three deosil circles above it with her hand, while visualizing blue-white light. She speaks words to the effect of:

Priestess: *"And I do bless and charge you to this work!"*

Next, the priestess cleanses the water, making three tuathail circles above it with her hand, while visualizing yellow-white light forcing out all negative energy. She speaks words to the effect of:

Priestess: *"Behold, I exorcise you, O creature of water, casting out from you any impurities that may lie within."*

Then she blesses the water, making three deosil circles above it with her hand, while visualizing blue-white light. She speaks words to the effect of:

Priestess: *"And I do bless and charge you to this work!"*

The priestess addresses the salt, saying:

Priestess: *"Behold, the salt is pure!"*

Then she addresses the water, saying:

Priestess: *"Behold, the water is pure!"*

The priestess now takes three pinches of salt and adds it to the water, saying as she does so something like this:

Priestess: *"Purity into purity then, and purity be blessed!"*

Taking the mixed salt and water, the priestess walks tuathail around the ritual space, aspersing the area as she goes. As she does this she should visualize yellow-white light filling the area and forcing out all negative or unfocused energy. As she asperses the area, the priestess may wish to say something like:

Priestess: *"I cleanse you . . . I cleanse you . . . I cleanse you . . ."*

When the priestess has finished aspersing, she returns the salt and water to the altar.

Now the priest turns to the token of fire. This will usually be either lit charcoal or a book of matches. (Refer back to the First Degree lessons for other possibilities.)

The priest cleanses the charcoal (or matches), making three tuathail circles above it with his hand, while visualizing yellow-white light. He imagines the light forcing out all negative or unfocused energy from the charcoal, then speaks words to the effect of:

Priest: *"Behold, I exorcise you, O creature of fire, casting out from you any impurities that may lie within."*

The priest blesses the charcoal, making three deosil circles above it with his hand, while visualizing blue-white light. Then he speaks words to the effect of:

Priest: *"And I do bless and charge you to this work!"*

Then the priest turns to the token of air, usually either powdered or solid incense.

The priest now cleanses the incense, making three tuathail circles above it with his hand, while visualizing yellow-white light forcing out all negative energy. He speaks words to the effect of:

Priest: *"Behold, I exorcise you, O creature of air, casting out from you any impurities that may lie within."*

Then he blesses the incense, making three deosil circles above it with his hand, while visualizing blue-white light. He speaks words to the effect of:

Priest: *"And I do bless and charge you to this work!"*

Now the priest addresses the charcoal (or matches), saying:

Priest: *"Behold, the fire is pure!"*

Then he addresses the incense, saying:

Priest: *"Behold, the air is pure!"*

The priest now takes three pinches of powdered incense and sprinkles it onto the charcoal (or he lights the solid incense with a match), saying as he does so something like:

Priest: *"Purity into purity then, and purity be blessed!"*

Taking the burning incense, the priest now walks deosil around the ritual space, censing the area as he goes. As he does this, he should visualize blue-white light filling the area and charging its energy. As he censes the area, the priest may wish to say something like:

Priest: *"I charge you . . . I charge you . . . I charge you . . ."*

Either the priestess or the priest now takes up the athame, sacred tool of air, and faces the east. She points the athame outward, visualizing a beam of white light shooting from the athame's tip to what will be the outer edge of the magic circle. Beginning from the east, she makes a deosil circle, demarcating the border of the magic circle with a barrier of light. As she does so, she may say something like:

Priestess: *"Behold, I do cut apart a place between the realms of humankind and of the Mighty Ones, a circle of art to focus and contain the powers we shall raise herein!"*

• • • •

Fire

Here follows the portion of the ritual that is identified with fire: the invocation of the quarters, deities, and ancestors.

The quarters are now called, beginning in the east:

The priestess first asperses the quarter with the salt and water, visualizing the area suffused with yellow-white light. She says something like:

Priestess: *"By the powers of earth and water, I do cleanse and purify the quarter of the east."*

The priest then censes the quarter with the burning incense, visualizing the area suffused with blue-white light. He says:

Priest: *"By the powers of fire and air do I charge the quarter of the east."*

The quarter is now invoked. If you have many people, each quarter may be done by a different person. Here we will give the eastern and southern quarters to the priest,

the western and northern quarters to the priestess.

The priest raises his wand, sacred tool of fire, or he may use his arm if he prefers. As he raises his wand, he imagines a column of pure white light arising in the east, at the border of the circle. He should say something like:

East

Priest: *"Hail unto you, O guardians of the Watchtower of the East, powers of air and inspiration! We invoke you and ask you to be with us this night, to share with us your love, your guidance, and your inspiration. We pray that you will help us to open our minds and our eyes and strengthen our thoughts as we go forward this night. We bid you hail and welcome!"*

All: *"Hail and welcome!"*

The process is repeated for each quarter: aspersing, censing, and using the wand to draw up the pillar of light. At each quarter, the invocation varies in order to acknowledge the specific guardians of that quarter.

South

Priest: *"Hail unto you, O guardians of the Watchtower of the South, powers of fire and manifestation! We invoke you* and ask you to be with us this night, to share with us your love, your guidance, and your inspiration. We pray that you will help us to open our courage and passion and strengthen our resolve as we go forward this night. We bid you hail and welcome!"

All: *"Hail and welcome!"*

West

Priestess: *"Hail unto you, O guardians of the Watchtower of the West, powers of water and compassion! We invoke you and ask you to be with us this night, to share with us your love, your guidance, and your inspiration. We pray that you will help us to open our hearts and our emotions and strengthen our sensitivity as we go forward this night. We bid you hail and welcome!"*

All: *"Hail and welcome!"*

North

Priestess: *"Hail unto you, O guardians of the Watchtower of the North, powers of earth and integration! We invoke you and ask you to be with us this night, to share with us your love, your guidance, and your inspiration. We pray that you will help us to open our souls and*

our Higher Selves and strengthen our understanding as we go forward this night. We bid you hail and welcome!"

All: *"Hail and welcome!"*

Now it is time to invoke Deity. Since Esbats are lunar ceremonies, the Goddess is invoked first. In this case we shall invoke the Goddess not in any particular personal form, but in her archetype as Maiden.

The priestess raises her arms to call upon the Goddess:

Priestess: *"O Maiden Goddess, we do invoke you at this time of the new moon, when the waxing light carries our hopes forward! Joyful Maiden, Lady of Laughter, Mistress of All Arts—the sun and moon are your adornments, and the sky your mirror. Lady of Creativity, Playful One, bless us we pray, and share with us your qualities of inspiration, self-expression, and wonder! We bid you hail and welcome!"*

All: *"Hail and welcome!"*

The priestess—and everyone else—should visualize the Goddess entering the circle in a way that makes sense to them, perhaps by imagining the Goddess in human form, or as a shower of glittering light, or as a ball or tower of light appearing in the circle. As you gain facility, you will no longer have to visualize Deity, but will perceive its energy either as a vision or as a feeling.

You may or may not choose to invoke the God for a new moon, since this is a lunar observance. Many people do invoke the God, for balance. Others do not. Here we will invoke the God in his archetype of Hero God.

The priest raises his arms to call upon the God:

Priest: *"O Gentle God, hero and champion, friend and protector, you are the brother of the Maiden, her companion and her Other Self, Lord of the sun and Fire. Be with us we pray, and share with us your qualities of courage and passion. Help us to carry our dreams and hopes forward in this time of the new moon! We bid you hail and welcome!"*

All: *"Hail and welcome!"*

Now visualize the God entering the circle.

Finally, you may wish to invoke the ancestors. These can be your physical ancestors or your philosophical ancestors. Since you are Correllian clergy, you may also invoke the ancestors of the Tradition. These include not only the blood ancestors, such as Caroline Highcorrell, Mable Highcorrell, and LaVeda Lewis-Highcorrell, but also the Tradition's philosophical ancestors, such as Lydia Beckett and Charles Leland. The Correllian ancestors might be invoked like this:

Priestess: *"O mighty ancestors, beloved ones who have gone before, we invoke you and ask you to join us and to bless us! Ancestors of the Correllian Tradition, priestesses and priests, mothers and uncles of the lineage, spiritual family that aids and supports us—lend us your inspiration and your love, your guidance and your aid this night, we pray. Beloved ones, we bid you hail and welcome!"*

All: *"Hail and welcome!"*

You might choose to include a chant here, such as "We Are One":

"We are one, my Lady!
We are one, my Lord!
We are one together!
We are one!

We are one, my Lady!
We are one, my Lord!

We are one together!
We are one!

We are one, my Lady!
We are one, my Lord!
We are one together!
We are one!"

• • • •
Spirit

Here you should discuss the nature of the Esbat gathering. You might say something such as:

"We come together tonight to celebrate the Esbat of the new moon. From now until the full moon, the lunar energies will wax and grow stronger. We attune ourselves to this energy, that our hopes and goals may grow stronger during this period as well. Now is the time of the Maiden Goddess, Lady of creativity and self-expression. Let us call upon our own creativity in this, our undertaking!"

• • • •
Act of Power
Lunar Energy/Burning

Here follows the part of the ritual that is identified with Spirit, the magical working or act of power.

This is the space for the body of the ritual itself. An act of power—a spell, a visualization, sometimes even the enactment of a mystery play—will follow here. This act of power is intended to attune to the energy of the waxing moon, and to repair the aura and reinvigorate the energetic system.

At the end of this section we will include two other examples of acts of power you might use for a new moon Esbat. We will do this at the end of each section, so that you have three examples of acts of power for each Esbat and Sabbat. But it is important to remember that these are just examples. Potential acts of power are limited only by your creativity and skill—and the more variety you employ in creating and implementing them, the better.

For this act of power you may wish to close your eyes or you may wish to leave your eyes open, whatever way is easiest for you to visualize. If you are outside and can actually see the new moon's crescent in the sky, use that image. You might lead the visualization like this:

*"Imagine the crescent of the
new moon above you.*

*Holy Maiden, at this time of the
new moon we ask you to help us to
attune to your energy. Give us the
gift of your essence, that we may
grow even as your light waxes."*

Imagine a beam of clear white light coming down from the moon, entering your body through the crown chakra and going into your heart. Let the moon's light form a ball of light in your heart chakra: clear, beautiful white light, pure and vibrant and full of strength and joy.

As more and more light enters you, let the ball of light in your heart chakra begin to fill your body. See it expanding slowly through your chest, through your limbs, filling you, suffusing you. Imagine the light beginning to expand beyond your body, moving out beyond the borders of your body—a few inches at first, then a few more, then about three feet in every direction, to form a ball of light all around you. Strong, clear, beautiful white light.

This is your aura. Feel the edges of your aura for holes or tears. If you find any, take a moment to seal them with the white light.

Now, coming down the beam of light from the moon, imagine another wave of energy. This energy is also white but filled with tiny, glittering stars of every color imaginable. Let the energy with its multicolored stars fill you. Let it fill your aura, more and more of it, until you are full of tiny glittering stars.

Then, coming down from the moon, feel another wave of energy. This is white light filled with silver stars. Let it enter through your crown chakra and fill you, the glittering silver stars swirling within you. Let it fill your aura. As more and more of the light enters, the multicolored stars become obscured, and soon all you can see are the silver stars. Then they become denser, fuller and fuller until at length you seem to be filled with a potent silver glitter, swirling and moving within you, scintillating and sparkling.

Now imagine the beam of light from the moon disappearing. Give thanks to the Goddess for this gift of her energy.

Now let the image fade. Keep what energy you need and release the rest into the earth, allowing it to flow out through the soles of your feet."

· · · ·

We will now continue with a second act of power. Although it is used here in conjunction with our lunar visualization, it could just as easily stand on its own.

This act of power is a burning intended to bring about a specific goal. This can be a single goal shared by the entire group, or each person may have an individual goal.

Begin by having everyone focus strongly on a goal or desire that they wish to bring to fruition either during this lunar cycle or over a longer period of time. Concentrate upon this goal. Imagine it as strongly as possible. Visualize the goal accomplished successfully.

Every person present should be given a small piece of paper, and a pen should be passed around from one person to the next. Let everyone write their goal upon the paper. Preferably this goal should be phrased in just one or two words. Remember to keep your goals positive, and aimed for the good of all.

Have a burning dish handy, either on the altar or in the middle of the circle. Have a candle burning in the dish or just next to it.

After everyone has written down their goal, begin to chant and dance deosil around the circle. As everyone dances, they should envision white light filling the circle, especially the burning dish.

Repeat the chant three times or continue as long as desired. Chants are best when they are simple, so that those who may be unfamiliar with the chants can quickly pick them up. A suitable chant here might be:

"Around the fire I dance a ring
Around the fire I dance and sing

Around the fire beneath the moon
I'll work my will to gain my boon!"

When the chant ends, have everyone light their piece of paper from the candle and deposit it in the burning dish. Instruct everyone to focus white light into the dish as it burns and to concentrate upon their goal. To this the presiding cleric might add a prayer on behalf of the group, such as:

"Behold, even as this paper burns
do we release our goals into
manifestation. May they burn as
brightly in the world as they do
here in the fire! As the moon's
light waxes, may Our Lady carry
these goals forward to fruition.
Divine Mother Goddess, Divine
Father God, beloved ancestors,
we pray that you will lend your
aid to this! So mote it be!"

All: *"So mote it be!"*

Then the presiding cleric should focus all of the energy into the burning dish, using her or his hands to symbolically guide it in and visualizing divine light coming into the burning dish as well.

"Behold, even as we have willed,
it is. These things have already
taken shape in the astral plane;

*now we shall allow them to
manifest in the physical plane."*

(Of course, that's not to say that a difficult goal may not have to be worked on more than once, but each time helps to draw it into manifestation. Also, you must accept it in order to receive it. If your mind wants it but your heart does not, for example, you will have a difficult time creating it.)

· · · ·
Water

Here follows the part of the ritual identified with the chalice, the blessing and sharing of the ritual toast.

Here you will bless the chalice and/or the food you will share. These are often termed "cakes and ale," but the term is purely ceremonial. "Cakes" are most often crackers, candies, slices of fruit, or—as we will represent them here—cookies.

You can put whatever you choose in the chalice, but you should be conscious of the preferences of those who will be present. Although a nice wine in the chalice can be good and wine is considered to be sacred, representing the lifeblood of the earth, for various reasons not everyone can partake of wine. Fruit juice can be just as good, and water is certainly just as representative of the life force. Here we will represent the chalice as bearing juice.

It is traditional to share the chalice itself, passing it from person to person around the circle; this is called a "loving cup." However, many people today prefer to pass out paper cups, especially if it is a large group, and bless a pitcher rather than a chalice per se. From the pitcher, the drink is then dispensed to the paper cups around the circle. Such a pitcher is still termed a "chalice."

Here is a simple way to bless the chalice. This is usually done by the priestess. Draw down divine energy into the chalice, visualized as white light coming down and filling the cup and radiating out from it as if it were a sun within. Say something like:

Priestess: *"Behold, in the name of the Goddess and the God, may this cup of love be blessed. As we share it, may it be as a bond between us, a token of the love we bear for them, and they for us, and we all for each other! So mote it be!"*

All: *"So mote it be!"*

Next, bless the cookies. This is often done by the priest. Draw down divine energy into the plate of cookies, again visualized as white light coming down and filling the plate, shining out from it like a sun within. Say something like:

Priest: *"Behold, in the name of the Goddess and the God may this produce of* the earth be blessed. As we share it, may we be refreshed, sustained, and strengthened. So mote it be!"

All: *"So mote it be!"*

Next, pass out the juice and cookies to all present, waiting until everyone has theirs.

Now offer the toast:

Priestess *(raises her cup):* *"To the Goddess!"*

All *(all raise their cups):* *"To the Goddess!"*

Priest *(raises his cookie):* *"To the God!"*

All *(all raise their cookies):* *"To the God!"*

Priestess: *"To us!"*

All: *"To us!"*

The juice and cookies may now be consumed.

After the toast is a good time for any announcements that need to be made, since everyone is still very focused. But it is usually best not to use this time for socializing, as this tends to bring down the energy in the circle.

Earth

Here follows the part of the ritual identified with earth, giving thanks and closing what has been opened.

Now you will close the ceremony and open the circle.

Begin by giving thanks to the ancestors and the deities.

Priestess: *"Beloved ancestors, you who have gone before, your wisdom and your example guide us. We pray that you will be with us and aid us as we go forward, that we may call upon the strength and knowledge of the past, even as we build the future. We thank you for your presence and your aid this night and at all times. May you blessed be in all things. We offer you our love and our respect! We bid you hail and farewell!"*

All: *"Hail and farewell!"*

Priest: *"Young Lord of the Sun, Hero and Champion, Friend and Protector, your courage and your devotion inspire us! We pray that you will be with us and aid us as we go forward, that even as the sun rises at dawn we too may rise and show our light to the world! We thank you for your presence and your aid this night, and at all times. We offer* you our love, and our respect! We bid you hail and farewell!"

All: *"Hail and farewell!"*

Priestess: *"O Maiden Goddess, Lady of the waxing moon, Mistress of beginnings and of growth, your joy and your creativity enliven us! We pray that you will be with us and aid us as we go forward, that even as the moon's light grows, we too may grow and shine forth as perfect expressions of God/Goddess. We thank you for your presence and your aid this night, and at all times. We offer you our love and our respect! We bid you hail and farewell!"*

All: *"Hail and farewell!"*

Next, thank each quarter. Start in the north.

North

Priestess: *"Hail unto you, O guardians of the Watchtower of the North, powers of earth and integration! We thank you for your presence here this night. May there be peace between us, now and always. Stay if you will, go if you must. We bid you hail and farewell!"*

All: *"Hail and farewell!"*

Using the wand, pull down the tower of white light that was erected when the north was called.

West

Priestess: *"Hail unto you, O guardians of the Watchtower of the West, powers of water and compassion! We thank you for your presence here this night. May there be peace between us, now and always. Stay if you will, go if you must. We bid you hail and farewell!"*

All: *"Hail and farewell!"*

Using the wand, pull down the tower of white light that was erected when the west was called.

South

Priest: *"Hail unto you, O guardians of the Watchtower of the South, powers of fire and manifestation! We thank you for your presence here this night. May there be peace between us, now and always. Stay if you will, go if you must. We bid you hail and farewell!"*

All: *"Hail and farewell!"*

Using the wand, pull down the tower of white light that was erected when the south was called.

East

Priest: *"Hail unto you, O guardians of the Watchtower of the East, powers of air and inspiration! We thank you for your presence here this night. May there be peace between us, now and always. Stay if you will, go if you must. We bid you hail and farewell!"*

All: *"Hail and farewell!"*

Using the wand, pull down the tower of white light that was erected when the east was called.

The presiding cleric, here presented as the priestess, now takes up her athame and points it toward the eastern quarter. She devokes the circle, walking tuathail. As she does this, she imagines the magic circle disappearing, the light returning back into the tip of the athame. As she opens the circle, she might use the popular formula:

Priestess: *"Behold: As above, so below! As the universe, so the soul! As within, so without! May the circle be open, but never broken! Merry meet, merry part, and merry meet again!"*

Finally, again cleanse and release all excess energy.

It is often the custom to follow the ritual with a feast, even if only a simple one.

This allows everyone time to wind down and helps everyone to ground thoroughly (eating food is itself a grounding act). I like to term it "the edible portion of our presentation." The feast provides social time for people, when they can get better acquainted and also discuss non-ritual topics. Some people like to discuss personal issues in circle, usually just before or just after sharing the chalice; we, however, have found it better to let discussion wait until the feast and to keep ritual for ritual.

• • • •

Variations

The foregoing is a sample of how one might do a new moon Esbat. To help you have a fuller idea of some of the many ways that this ritual can be done, I am also including some variations on the theme of visualizations and acts of power.

This is only a very narrow sampling of the potential variations you might employ. The idea is to attune to the energy of the new moon for growth and increase—the ways to do this are endless. There are many, many books available from which you can glean ideas for ritual. Never be afraid to improvise. Remember that ritual is an expression of the heart. Moreover, as you gain practice and facility you will find that you prefer or excel in certain techniques more than others, and you will want to make full use of these.

21

Above all, remember that in order to be effective, a ritual must raise energy. It should be a moving and enjoyable experience. Therefore, always strive to keep it fresh and innovative.

Here are several examples of other acts of power that you might use in a new moon Esbat. Do not, by any means, feel limited by these examples. They are only meant to inspire you. The potential choices of acts of power that you might use in a ritual are endless, bounded only by your creativity and skill. Ideally, as you gain experience you will amass a large number of acts of power for use in ritual, which you will adapt to the needs of each individual ceremony. Never be afraid of innovation or variety, because it is important always to keep the ritual experience fresh.

· · · ·

Act of Power #2
World Tree Visualization

"Close your eyes: relax and go inside yourself. Become aware of your heart chakra, and imagine a ball of white light within it. This is the light of the Eternal Flame, your connection to Goddess—the Divine Spark within you. In this ball of light is love and peace and strength. Feel the love and power in the light—the love of the Goddess.

Now imagine that ball of white light expanding. See it grow larger, filling your chest. Imagine it growing to fill your torso, moving out farther to encompass your arms and legs. See the ball of light expanding beyond your body, to form a ball of light around you. Feel the energy of the light; feel it surrounding you; feel it suffusing you. You are safe in the ball of light, for it is the light of the Goddess, and in it are strength and love and peace.

Relax. Feel yourself floating within the ball of light. Let the ball of light lift you, carry you. Feel yourself rising up, gently carried by the ball of light, supported by the love of the Goddess.

Imagine that you are floating, gently carried along by the night breeze. Comfortable. Safe. Supported by the love of the Goddess.

The earth is far below and the stars are all around you. Below you see buildings, roads, trees, and rivers, but they are all far away from you. You are simply, peacefully floating.

Consider your life for a moment now that you are far from it, floating in the sky. What is important to you at this point in life? Think of a goal that you wish to work for, something that you want to develop or to do, something that you want to see prosper. Concentrate upon your goal. Imagine the goal strongly.

Imagine the ball of light coming down to Earth now. Imagine it coming to a rest in a clearing in the woods. The image of the ball of light fades from around you, but its protection remains. Look about you. What do you see? What is the condition of the woods? How does it make you feel?

Imagine yourself forming a ball of light between your two hands: a ball of clear, white light. In that ball, imagine your goal fulfilled. See the goal accomplished, within the ball of light that is

between your hands. Focus and concentrate upon your goal.

Now you will see a seed appear at the center of the ball of light between your hands. A single seed, glowing with light as if a tiny sun were within it.

Make a little hole in the soil before you, and plant the seed. Cover it over and look into the sky above you. There you will see the first sliver of the waxing crescent moon. Speak to her. Ask her to send down her light upon your seed.

Now imagine a shower of white light raining down from the new moon, and in the white light are millions of tiny, glittering silver stars. It only lasts a few moments, but it is indescribably beautiful, scintillating with energy.

In front of you, you see a tiny shoot poke up through the ground. The shoot stretches upward, slowly growing into a sapling. As you watch, the sapling grows into a tree.

The tree grows larger and larger. It grows taller than you. Then it grows taller than you can see. The branches of the tree spread out above you, reaching out in every direction, full of green leaves.

And in the tree you begin to see living things. Birds, animals—every kind of animal. Small animals you would expect to see in a tree like squirrels, big animals that you would not expect to see in a tree, like water buffalo. Aquatic creatures, too, seemingly out of place. And people, all kinds of people throughout the branches of the tree. For this is the Tree of Life, and all life is in the Tree.

And moving through the branches of the tree, you perceive the Great Dragon, Uktena, the Ourobouros, the Tao, the movement of creation. It is too big for you to truly see it, yet you feel it and catch glimpses of it among the branches.

And then up among the branches, you see it, your goal. Fulfilled and successful, the goal appears already accomplished in the branches of the tree. Claim it as your own. Accept and give thanks for it.

Now you see the glittering light of the new moon begin to shine through the branches of the tree, white with millions of tiny, glittering stars sparkling throughout it. The light shines brighter and brighter. It spreads out from the tree. It suffuses everything. You are engulfed in the glittering white light. It is all you can see. It fills you completely. And in the light is love and joy and peace . . .

And the image fades. You return slowly to yourself. On the count of three, you are back. One: slowly returning to the body. Two: a little more, almost there. Three: you are back, refreshed and invigorated."

This visualization is not only intended as a spell to help you magically create your goal, but as a divination as well.

What was the clearing in the woods like when the ball of light first deposited you there? Was it healthy and thriving or barren? This represents how you actually feel about your goal. If the clearing was not healthy and thriving, examine your feelings about the goal and look for crossed wires, mixed feelings that may tend to trip you up or lead to self-sabotage. When you find them, change them and reprogram them.

And what did the tree look like? This indicates how your goal will grow. Was it tall and straight? Was it interestingly gnarled? Was it healthy and verdant? How did it make you feel? If you do not like the answers to these questions, you may re-imagine the tree later and send it healing energy. Visualize it healed and healthy.

• • • •

Act of Power #3
Group Divination

Our final act of power for this section is a divination intended to determine how the month will go for the individuals present (or a longer period of time, if desired).

For this, you will need a tarot deck (or another form of divination such as rune stones).

Pass the deck around the circle and let everyone draw one card, which they should not look at yet. This card will represent what the month holds for this person.

Now pass the deck around a second time. This time, as each person receives the deck, interpret the first card they drew; again, this is what the month holds for them. For example, the Chariot might be taken to represent achieving goals, while

the Seven of Cups indicates confusion or misunderstandings.

Next, ask each person to draw another card and pass the deck on. Again, they should not look at the new card.

Send the deck around a third time. As each person receives the deck, interpret the second card that each person drew. This card represents their interactions with the group in circle. For example, the Ace of Cups suggests happy relations and the Three of Swords suggests that the person may have a falling out of some sort.

Now ask everyone to draw another card and to pass the deck on around the circle.

When everyone has drawn their third card, you will not pass the deck around again. Instead, you will go around and in-terpret each card. This card represents the person's relationship with the world outside of the circle. For example, the Seven of Wands suggests achievement through hard work, while the Five of Swords suggests dissatisfaction with present circumstances.

Chapter

III

Full Moon Esbats

For most Wiccans, the full moon Esbat is the most important of the monthly ceremonies, and in many temples it is the only one observed. This is when we honor the power of the Mother Goddess, symbolized by the moon and acknowledge our connection to her. It is also a prime time for magical workings.

It is no wonder that the full moon has always been the subject of worship. In ancient times, and still today, if one was far from city lights, the full moon lit up the nocturnal landscape almost as brightly as the sun lights the day. The connection between the lunar cycle and women's menstrual cycles, the ebb and flow of the tides, and the behaviors of animals gave rise to the concept of correspondences, through which we humans learned to interpret all things, and also to the concept of sympathetic magic that has been with us since the dawn of time.

Today, at least for those of us who live in cities, the magic and mystery of the full moon is greatly diminished by the eternal presence of electric light, which drowns out the gentler influence of moonlight. We may be struck by the beauty of the full moon, but the full effect of its grandeur can only be observed in the countryside.

There is an ancient custom that many people still observe, of kissing the back of their hand when they first see the moon at night, especially the full moon. This act acknowledges that the moon is a symbol of the Goddess, but the Goddess truly dwells within.

At the new moon, people seek to align themselves with the growing energies of the waxing moon, so that they and their goals will grow in the same way. So, too, at the full moon people seek to align themselves with the lunar energies, which are here at their height, and use these energies as a kind of battery to further their magical workings.

We've all heard the stories of how hospitals and police stations are busiest at the full moon, that many people become unusually agitated at the full moon, and that people who are emotionally disturbed tend to become more so at this time. Dreams are often more vivid and more easily remembered during the full moon, and nightmares (in which the self confronts its major issues) are more common at this time. This is because the lunar cycle effects our psychic energies, and when the moon is full we have more energy than at other times—too much energy for some people. For some people, this extra energy just leaves them ungrounded and excitable, but for the magic worker it makes the raising and directing of energy that much easier, since the energy is already heightened to begin with.

It is also worth bearing in mind that the astrological sign the full moon is in will tend to color the energy: for example, a full moon in Scorpio will tend to emphasize emotional issues and also issues around dominance. This is easy to keep track of, however; just as the dark moon/new moon occurs when the moon is in conjunction with the sun, so too the full moon occurs when the moon is in opposition to the sun—that is to say, when the sun and moon are directly opposite each other. Symbolically, this represents the independence and power of the Goddess at her height during the full moon. The cycle also corresponds to the creation story, beginning with the Goddess and God (moon and sun) united as one, then continuing through their separation and ending when they return to union again.

Because the full moon is the opposition of moon and sun, the full moon will always be in the astrological sign exactly opposite from the one the sun is in, so it is easy to calculate. Thus:

> If the sun is in Aries, the full moon will be in Libra.
>
> If the sun is in Taurus, the full moon will be in Scorpio.
>
> If the sun is in Gemini, the full moon will be in Sagittarius.
>
> If the sun is in Cancer, the full moon will be in Capricorn.
>
> If the sun is in Leo, the full moon will be in Aquarius.
>
> If the sun is in Virgo, the full moon will be in Pisces.
>
> If the sun is in Libra, the full moon will be in Aries.
>
> If the sun is in Scorpio, the full moon will be in Taurus.
>
> If the sun is in Sagittarius, the full moon will be in Gemini.
>
> If the sun is in Capricorn, the full moon will be in Cancer.
>
> If the sun is in Aquarius, the full moon will be in Leo.
>
> If the sun is in Pisces, the full moon will be in Virgo.

Here then is a basic Esbat ceremony to celebrate the full moon, together with several examples of possible variations upon the main body of the ritual. Remember that this is only a template—a sample upon which to build your own rituals. Adapt it to your needs and never be afraid to innovate and expand upon what you have learned. This is how we grow, and life is growth.

As in the new moon Esbat, we begin with a formal Correllian circle casting:

. . . .

Air

Begin by clearing and releasing all excess energy, as usual. Release all tensions and anxieties; just let them flow through and out of your body like a gentle wave of energy, exiting through the soles of your feet.

The priestess cleanses the salt, making three tuathail circles above it with her hand, while visualizing yellow-white light. She imagines the light forcing out all negative or unfocused energy from the salt. She speaks words to the effect of:

Priestess: *"Behold, I exorcise you, O creature of earth, casting out from you any impurities that may lie within."*

Then the priestess blesses the salt, making three deosil circles above it with her hand while visualizing blue-white light. She speaks words to the effect of:

Priestess: *"And I do bless and charge you to this work!"*

Next the priestess cleanses the water, making three tuathail circles above it with her hand while visualizing yellow-white light forcing out all negative energy. She speaks words to the effect of:

Priestess: *"Behold, I exorcise you, O creature of water, casting out from you any impurities that may lie within."*

Then she blesses the water, making three deosil circles above it with her hand while visualizing blue-white light. She speaks words to the effect of:

Priestess: *"And I do bless and charge you to this work!"*

The priestess addresses the salt, saying:

Priestess: *"Behold, the salt is pure!"*

Then she addresses the water, saying:

Priestess: *"Behold, the water is pure!"*

The priestess now takes three pinches of salt and adds it to the water, saying as she does so something like:

Priestess: *"Purity into purity then, and purity be blessed!"*

Taking the mixed salt and water, the priestess walks tuathail around the ritual space, aspersing the area as she goes. As she does this, she should visualize yellow-white light filling the area and forcing out all negative or unfocused energy. As she

asperses the area, the priestess may wish to say something to the effect of:

Priestess: *"I cleanse you . . . I cleanse you . . . I cleanse you . . . "*

When the priestess has finished aspersing, she returns the salt and water to the altar.

Now the priest turns to the token of fire. This will usually be either a lit charcoal or a book of matches. (Please refer back to the First Degree for other possibilities.)

The priest cleanses the charcoal (or matches), making three tuathail circles above it with his hand while visualizing yellow-white light. He imagines the light forcing out all negative or unfocused energy from the charcoal, and then speaks words such as:

Priest: *"Behold, I exorcise you, O creature of fire, casting out from you any impurities that may lie within."*

The priest blesses the charcoal, making three deosil circles above it with his hand while visualizing blue-white light. Then he speaks words to the effect of:

Priest: *"And I do bless and charge you to this work!"*

Then the priest turns to the token of air, usually either powdered or solid incense.

The priest now cleanses the incense, making three tuathail circles above it with his hand while visualizing yellow-white light forcing out all negative energy. He speaks words to the effect of:

Priest: *"Behold, I exorcise you, O creature of air, casting out from you any impurities that may lie within."*

Then he blesses the incense, making three deosil circles above it with his hand, while visualizing blue-white light. He speaks words to the effect of:

Priest: *"And I do bless and charge you to this work!"*

Now the priest addresses the charcoal (or matches), saying:

Priest: *"Behold, the fire is pure!"*

Then he addresses the incense, saying:

Priest: *"Behold, the air is pure!"*

The priest now takes three pinches of powdered incense and sprinkles it onto the charcoal (or lights the solid incense with a match), saying as he does so something like this:

Priest: *"Purity into purity then, and purity be blessed!"*

Taking the burning incense, the priest now walks deosil around the ritual space, censing the area as he goes. As he does this he should visualize blue-white light filling the area and charging its energy. As he censes the area, the priest may wish to say something like:

Priest: *"I charge you . . . I charge you . . . I charge you . . ."*

Either the priestess or the priest now takes up the athame, sacred tool of air, and faces the east. She points the athame outward, visualizing a beam of white light shooting from the athame's tip to what will be the outer edge of the magic circle. Beginning from the east, she makes a deosil circle, marking out the border of the magic circle with a barrier of light. As she does so, she may say something like:

Priestess: *"Behold, I do cut apart a place between the realms of humankind and of the Mighty Ones, a circle of art to focus and contain the powers we shall raise herein!"*

• • • •

Fire

The quarters are now called, beginning in the east:

The priestess first asperses the quarter with the salt and water, visualizing the area suffused with yellow-white light. She says something like:

Priestess: *"By the powers of earth and water, I do cleanse and purify the quarter of the east."*

The priest then censes the quarter with the burning incense, visualizing the area suffused with blue-white light. He says:

Priest: *"By the powers of fire and air do I charge the quarter of the east."*

The quarter is now invoked. If you have many people, each quarter may be done by a different person. Here we will give the eastern and southern quarters to the priest, the western and northern quarters to the priestess.

The priest raises his wand, sacred tool of fire, or he may use his arm if he prefers. As he raises his wand, he imagines a column of pure white light arising in the east, at the border of the circle. He should say something like:

East

Priest: *"Hail unto you, O guardians of the Watchtower of the East, powers of air and inspiration! We invoke you and ask you to be with us this night, to share with us your love, your guidance, and your inspiration. We pray that you*

will help us to open our minds and our eyes and strengthen our thoughts as we go forward this night. We bid you hail and welcome!"

All: *"Hail and welcome!"*

The process is repeated for each quarter, aspersing, censing, and using the wand to draw up the pillar of light. At each quarter, the invocation varies to acknowledge the specific guardians of that quarter.

South

Priest: *"Hail unto you, O guardians of the Watchtower of the South, powers of fire and manifestation! We invoke you, and ask you to be with us this night, to share with us your love, your guidance, and your inspiration. We pray that you will help us to open our courage and passion and strengthen our resolve as we go forward this night. We bid you hail and welcome!"*

All: *"Hail and welcome!"*

West

Priestess: *"Hail unto you, O guardians of the Watchtower of the West, powers of water and compassion! We invoke you and ask you to be with us this night, to share with us your love, your guidance,* and your inspiration. We pray that you will help us to open our hearts and our emotions and strengthen our sensitivity as we go forward this night. We bid you hail and welcome!"

All: "Hail and welcome!"

North

Priestess: "Hail unto you, O guardians of the Watchtower of the North, powers of earth and integration! We invoke you and ask you to be with us this night, to share with us your love, your guidance, and your inspiration. We pray that you will help us to open our souls and our Higher Selves and strengthen our understanding as we go forward this night. We bid you hail and welcome!"

All: "Hail and welcome!"

Now it is time to invoke Deity. Since Esbats are lunar ceremonies, the Goddess is invoked first. In this case we shall invoke the Goddess not in any particular personal form but in her archetype as Mother, although you could use whatever personal form you choose.

The priestess raises her arms to call upon the Goddess:

Priestess: "Divine Mother Goddess, All-Bountiful, All-Beautiful, Source and Sustenance of Existence, we do invoke you now in the time of the full moon, when the radiant symbol of your love shines above us in the heavens. Holy Mother, even as your moon lights the darkness of the earth below, may your Divine Love be as a light within our hearts, now and always! Light our path, guide and strengthen us, enfold us in your love, Divine Mother, we thus pray! Holy One, we bid you hail and welcome!"

All: "Hail and welcome!"

The priestess and everyone else should visualize the Mother Goddess entering the circle in a way that makes sense to them —perhaps by imagining the Goddess in human form, or as a shower of glittering light, or as a ball or tower of light appearing in the circle. As you gain facility you will no longer have to visualize the Deity, but will perceive its energy either as a vision or as a feeling.

Since the full moon is a lunar ceremony, you may or may not wish to invoke the God. As stated in chapter 2, some people do prefer to invoke the God in Esbat rites, some do not—the choice belongs to the celebrants. Here we will invoke the God in his archetype of Lover.

The priest raises his arms to call upon the God:

Priest: *"Holy Father God, Son, Brother, and Consort of Our Lady, we do invoke you now in the time of her glory. Born of her body, you dance the dance of life and death with her, following her steps as we follow yours, eternally reborn and renewed. As she spins the thread of life, you turn the Wheel. What she gives birth to, you give form to, O Lord of Time and Space. Be with us now, we pray. We bid you hail and welcome!"*

All: *"Hail and welcome!"*

If you choose to do so, you may now invoke the ancestors. Here we invoke the ancestors of the Correllian Tradition, although you might invoke your personal ancestors:

Priestess: *"O mighty ancestors, beloved ones who have gone before, we invoke you and ask you to join us and to bless us! Ancestors of the Correllian Tradition, priestesses and priests, mothers and uncles of the lineage, spiritual family that aids and supports us, lend us your inspiration and your love, your guidance and your aid this night, we*

pray. Beloved ones, we bid you hail and welcome!"

All: *"Hail and welcome!"*

• • • •
Spirit

Here you should discuss the nature of the Esbat gathering. You might say something like:

"We come together tonight to celebrate the Esbat of the full moon. Now the powers of the moon are at their height, and the monthly cycle of the psychic tide is at its strongest. We attune ourselves to this heightened energy, that we may use it to manifest our hopes and goals. Now is the time of the Mother Goddess, who creates and sustains all things. Let us call upon her bounty to aid us in this our undertaking!"

• • • •
Act of Power
Full Moon Visualization/Divination

What follows is the main body of the ritual. This is the place for an act of power, a spell, visualization, mystery play, or any combination of these elements.

In this case, our act of power is intended to draw upon the heightened energies of the full moon to help in manifesting personal goals. This same technique can be used for manifesting group goals, but if you choose to work on group goals, make sure everyone involved understands and agrees with those goals, so that the energy will be properly focused.

This act of power is a visualization. It can be done with eyes open or closed. If you happen to be outside and the full moon is visible, you might want to begin by having people gaze upon it for a few moments. Then lead the visualization, saying something along these lines:

"Imagine the face of the full moon. See her clearly in your mind— gaze upon her. Behold her soft luminance, her pearly light. Imagine her qualities. What do you feel from her? Love? Strength? Peace?

Feel her energy, commune with her. Bond with her.

Think about what it is that you most wish to have at this time. Hold it in your heart and whisper it to her. Confide in her. Tell her what you need and know that in doing so, you are telling the Goddess.

Divine Mother Goddess, hear the prayers of your children and clasp them to your bosom. From our heart to yours. We pray that you will aid us in manifesting that which we are working for this night. Share with us your energy, strongest at this time of the full moon. Strengthen us and lend your power to ours!

Now imagine a shower of soft white light descending from the moon upon the whole circle, like a gentle rain: beautiful, clear white light, full of strength and love. See the light descending upon each person all at once. See each person bathed in white light, filled with white light, the light of the Goddess. And feel it coming down upon you as well.

Feel the light coming down all around you, entering you through the top of your head, filling your body as water fills a bottle. Feel its purity, its strength, its strong vibration moving all through you. Bond with the light, be one with the light, be one with the Goddess.

35

*Focus on the light that fills
you. Concentrate on it. Feel
its texture, its movement.
Let it work within you.*

*Now raise your hands. Hold them
toward the center of the circle,
palms out. And through your palm
chakras, send forth a stream of
white light filled with tiny silver
stars. Send the white light with
silver stars into the center of
the circle, where everyone else is
sending theirs. Imagine a great
ball of this light forming there:
white light with swirling, sparkling,
glittering silver stars. The more
light you send into the ball of light
at the center of the circle, the
denser the silver stars become, until
at last you can see only the stars
in a great whirling ball of energy.*

*Inside that ball of energy, now
imagine again your goal, what
you wish to have. See it within
the ball of stars. Imagine it as
clearly as you can. See the goal
already accomplished, see yourself
having it and being happy with
it. Don't worry about how it will*

*be accomplished; just know that
it is already yours and will soon
take shape. Now chant with me:*

*I will it: it is!
I call it: it is!
I make it: it is!
I accept it: it is mine!*

*And see the ball of stars suddenly
disperse, like a great quicksilver
explosion—the energy flowing
out in all directions, carrying our
goals outward into manifestation, a
manifestation already accomplished
on the astral plane, which will begin
to take shape on the physical plane
as soon as the circle is opened.*

*Now let the energy dissipate.
Then clear and release any
excess energy you are holding."*

We will now continue with a second act
of power that, although it could also be
adapted and used on its own, is here intended to complete the body of our ritual.

The purpose of this act of power in
this context is to ascertain the extent to
which the visualization has been effective
in the manifesting of goals for each individual, and to tell each one either how they
may expect the goals to manifest (sudden

changes, prosperity, inner developments, and so on), or what they may need to do to assist the process of manifestation (take action, be patient, meditate, and so forth).

For this act of power you will need a bowl filled with lots. The lots may be in the form of slips of paper with particular messages written on them, such as "It will come out well," "Complete success," "Be patient and persevere," "Sudden happenings," and so on. Or they can be symbols that will be interpreted to give the message—for example, you could use different colored stones such as red for "immediate success," black for "delayed success," and gray for "it will work out differently from what you expect." Experiment and work out a system you like. The lots should allow for a number of different possibilities, including the possibility that things may take shape differently than expected, but they should all be positive and reflect different ways for the spell to work out based upon the knowledge that it absolutely *will* work one way or another. There should not be a "no" answer, although answers like "Continue to manifest" or "Fine-tune your idea" are okay.

Pass the bowl around. Ask each person to think of the goal they have just worked for and select a lot. Then go around and interpret the lots.

Although we have presented it here as a companion divination whose purpose is to detect how well a previous manifestation has worked, this act of power may also be done as an independent divination. When used as an independent divination, each person would ask a question and the answer be interpreted. In that case, it would be appropriate to include "no" answers.

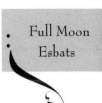

• • • •

Water

Now it is time for the toast, and I include here a different and more complex example of how the toast might be done. As always, it is only an example from which you may develop your own ideas.

For this toast, you will need two different liquids: one dark and one light—for example, red grape juice and white grape juice. The priestess will take the darker drink, the priest the lighter one. You will also need a large chalice or a pitcher, and paper cups if you prefer.

This version of the toast includes only the drink and no food.

The priestess will begin; she can say something like:

Priestess: "*In the Beginning was the Goddess, and she was alone and without form. She was the first Darkness, and she slept alone in the boundless sea that was before creation. Yet as she slept, she dreamed. And from her*

37

dreams came ideas and desires. And she came to know that she desired more. And so she created the God."

Priest: "And the God came forth in a blast of light and fire, where before there had only been darkness. As the Goddess was Darkness, he was Light. As the Goddess was Yin, he was Yang. He danced for joy at the moment of creation, and his heart burned with the beauty that was life."

Priestess: "And the Goddess saw that the God was beautiful. And she desired to be one with him again. She sought counsel of her Higher Self, and was told 'To rise you must fall.' This meant that she could not bring the God back into her, but to unite with him she must enter into the physical world that he had become."

Priest: "And so the Goddess separated off the many souls from herself. They were as her children, yet they were also her selves for she herself was the spark of light within them. And she sent the souls into the physical world and placed them into physical forms, and thus Goddess became one with God again."

The priestess raises her bottle and imagines it filled with the divine energy shining out in all directions.

Priestess: "Behold, in the name of the Goddess, may this wine be blessed." [Note: It is okay to call it wine even if you're using fruit juice; the term is symbolic.]

The priest now raises his bottle and likewise imagines it filled with the divine energy, shining out in all directions.

Priest: "Behold, in the name of the God, may this wine be blessed."

The priestess and priest now pour their two beverages simultaneously into the chalice or pitcher, uniting them even as the Goddess and God are united through the miracle of Incarnation.

Priestess and priest together: "Behold, we are jointly blessed."

Priestess: "Behold, may this cup of love be as a bond between ourselves and the Goddess and God, from whose Divine Love we and all things proceed, and also between us and one another, united in perfect love and perfect trust here within this circle."

Pass the chalice around the circle, or pass out paper cups and take the pitcher around the circle to fill them according to preference.

. . . .

Earth

Next, you will close the ceremony and open the circle.

Begin by giving thanks to the ancestors and the deities.

Priestess: *"Beloved ancestors, you who have gone before, your wisdom and your example guide us. We pray that you will be with us and aid us as we go forward, that we may call upon the strength and knowledge of the past, even as we build the future. We thank you for your presence and your aid this night and at all times. May you blessed be in all things. We offer you our love and our respect! We bid you hail and farewell!"*

All: *"Hail and farewell!"*

Priestess: *"Divine Father God, Son, Brother, and Consort of Our Lady. You are the Lord of the Dance, Master of Time and Space. You give form to what she creates, and turn the Wheel that life may progress forward. We thank you for your presence and your aid this*

night and at all times. We offer you our love and our respect! We bid you hail and farewell!"

All: *"Hail and farewell!"*

Priestess: *"Divine Mother Goddess, Lady of the full moon, Mother and Mistress of Existence. You are the source and sustenance of all life! Your love lights our path through darkness, and your wisdom guides us on our walk through life. You care for us as a Mother for her children—for truly you are our Divine Mother! We thank you for your presence and your aid this night and at all times. We offer you our love and our respect! We bid you hail and farewell!"*

All: *"Hail and farewell!"*

Now thank each quarter. Start in the north.

North

Priestess: *"Hail unto you, O guardians of the Watchtower of the North, powers of earth and integration! We thank you for your presence here this night. May there be peace between us, now and always. Stay if you will, go if you must. We bid you hail and farewell!"*

All: *"Hail and farewell!"*

Using the wand, pull down the tower of white light that was erected when the north was called.

West

Priestess: *"Hail unto you, O guardians of the Watchtower of the West, powers of water and compassion! We thank you for your presence here this night. May there be peace between us, now and always. Stay if you will, go if you must. We bid you hail and farewell!"*

All: *"Hail and farewell!"*

Using the wand, pull down the tower of white light that was erected when the west was called.

South

Priest: *"Hail unto you, O guardians of the Watchtower of the South, powers of fire and manifestation! We thank you for your presence here this night. May there be peace between us, now and always. Stay if you will, go if you must. We bid you hail and farewell!"*

All: *"Hail and farewell!"*

Using the wand, pull down the tower of white light that was erected when the south was called.

East

Priest: *"Hail unto you, O guardians of the Watchtower of the East, powers of air and inspiration! We thank you for your presence here this night. May there be peace between us, now and always. Stay if you will, go if you must. We bid you hail and farewell!"*

All: *"Hail and farewell!"*

Using the wand, pull down the tower of white light that was erected when the east was called.

Now the presiding cleric, here presented as the priestess, takes up her athame and points it toward the eastern quarter. She devokes the circle, walking tuathail. As she does this, she imagines the magic circle disappearing, the light returning back into the tip of the athame. As she opens the circle, she might say:

Priestess: *"Behold: As above, so below! As the universe, so the soul! As within, so without! May the circle be open but never broken! Merry meet, merry part, and merry meet again!"*

Finally, again cleanse and release all excess energy.

. . . .

Variations

I am including two other examples of possible acts of power, which might be used in a full moon Esbat. Of course these are only examples—there are many similar examples that could be used, and you should learn how to create your own as well. Remember, ritual is not about the repetition of other people's example, but it is an expression of spirituality that should flow freely through the ritual participants. Never be afraid to listen to your own inner voice.

. . . .

Act of Power #2
Healing Circle

This visualization is a healing circle. It can be used to send healing energy to people, plants or animals, places, situations, or even the earth itself—in this example we use it for people. The technique can be used as it is here—as part of a larger ceremony—or it can be used by itself.

This visualization may be done with eyes open or closed, depending on which way is easiest for you.

It should be noted that even healing energy should never be forced upon anyone. Thus the visualization offers the subject's Higher Self the choice to accept or reject the healing (a choice the Higher Self has in any event, whether or not it is stated). If the Higher Self rejects the healing, it simply will not take the energy, and the energy will return to the earth.

You might lead the visualization this way:

"Let us begin by clearing and releasing all excess energy. Let it pour out of us like a wave, down through our feet and into the earth to be reused for other purposes.

Now let us become aware of our heart chakras. Imagine a ball of clear white light in your heart chakra—beautiful, clear white light, shining within your chest like a sun. Within the ball of light, feel peace and strength and love—the love of the Goddess. Let that love and peace radiate within you, filling you with strength and tranquillity.

Now imagine a column of pure white light rising up from the earth in the very center of the circle. A tall column—about three feet wide of clear, strong white light—like the towers we raise at the quarters.

*Feel the ball of light in your
heart chakra: feel the peace and
tranquillity, the strength and
protection radiating from it. From
that ball of light—from your
heart chakra—send forth a beam
of green light to the column of
light in the center of the circle.
This will be the channel for our
healing energy to flow through.*

*Now we will go around the circle,
and each person may name
someone to be put inside the column
for healing. Then we will chant
that person's name three times."*

Here you will go around the circle, one
person at a time. When it is their turn, each
person may name one person to be healed.
If they wish, they may name themselves.
You can go around the circle as many times
as you like, but it's best not to overdo it.

Let us say that our first subject for healing is named Helen:

*"Let us chant Helen's
name three times:*

*Helen!
Helen!
Helen!*

*Imagine Helen in the column of
light. You don't have to know what
she looks like —imagine her,
however her image comes to you.*

*From your heart send healing
energy to Helen—send healing
energy from your heart through
the green beam of light and into
the column: see it go to Helen's
heart. See the healing light fill her,
suffuse her; imagine her shining
with bright, healing light."*

Now address Helen's Higher Self.

*"Helen, we ask you to accept this
healing energy if you would. It is
your choice, in accordance with
your free will. Use the energy for
your highest good. Helen, we ask
you to accept this energy and heal,
now, in this moment—become
whole, healthy, and happy.'*

*And imagine Helen receiving the
energy, see her become whole,
healthy, and happy. See her illness
or her burdens drop away and
see her become vibrant, joyful,
and filled with healing energy.*

*Divine Mother Goddess, Divine
Father God, we pray that you will
be with Helen, and that you will
help her in any way she needs in
order to accomplish her highest
good in the best possible manner!*

*Now let the image fade, and let
us proceed to the next person."*

Proceed to the next person, who will
name a subject to be healed, and repeat the
same procedure for the new subject. Continue on around the circle this way, moving
person to person in a clockwise manner,
until everyone has had a chance.

*"Now let us imagine all of the
people to whom we have sent
healing energy together in the circle.
See them all healthy, healed, and
happy. We will chant the word
heal three times and send them
a final dose of healing energy.*

*Heal!
Heal!
Heal!*

*And from your heart send forth
healing energy through the green
beam of light and into the column.*

*See the healing energy go to
all these people, bringing them
strength and health and joy. We
say to you all: Be healed and made
whole. Be healthy and joyful. We
pray that all of you shall have all
you need to complete your highest
good in the best ways possible.
Divine Mother Goddess, Divine
Father God, we pray that you will
be with all of these people and help
them in every way they need!*

*And see all the people just that
much happier and healthier,
guided by the love of the Divine,
shining and radiating with light.*

Now let the image fade.

*And finally, let us put the
earth in the column of light.
Imagine the earth in the
column of light. Let us chant
her name three times:*

*Earth!
Earth!
Earth!*

*And from your heart send forth
healing energy through the beam*

of green light to Mother Earth.
See her receive the energy—
see it fill her. See the earth
whole and healthy and happy,
shining with healing light.

Mother Earth, we ask you to accept
this healing energy and use it as
you see fit. We pray that you may
be healed and made whole. We
say to you, Mother Earth: heal
now! Divine Mother Goddess,
Divine Father God, may it be so!

And see the earth healed and
healthy and happy, shining
and vibrant with healing light,
refreshed and revitalized—her
hurts healed, her burdens eased.

Now let the image fade.

Pull back the beam of green
light into your heart.
Imagine the column of light sink
back down into the earth."

. . . .

Act of Power #3
Cone of Power

Our next act of power is an important
magical technique called the *cone of power*.

This is a basic technique that is often used
in ritual, usually accompanied by dancing in a deosil circle. We offer it here as a
visualization to help you to become familiar with its mechanics. Once you can do
this easily as a visualization, you should
try it with dance; as the celebrants dance
in a circle, they imagine the cone of power
building as in the visualization below, then
release the cone just as the dance stops.

The cone of power may be used as an
energetic vehicle for any goal: either individual goals or a single group goal. Here we
treat the group as having individual goals,
known only to themselves. You might begin like this:

"Let us begin by joining hands.

Take a moment to focus upon your
goal. See it clearly. Concentrate
on it strongly. Focus your magical
intent upon the goal. Imagine
it fulfilled. Be clear about the
goal; know that it is yours.

Now imagine a small ball of white
energy in your left hand. Feel it;
imagine the heat of the energy
in your hand, the intensity of it.
Imagine it, clear and white, shining,
strong and filled with power.

Now imagine in your right hand a similar ball of energy, not your own but generated by the person to your right. Feel it as strongly as you feel your own ball of energy. Feel its strength and power. Imagine it clearly, bright and white and unclouded.

Now imagine the energy from the ball in your right hand beginning to move toward your left—slowly, slowly—until there is a solid cord of energy between your two hands, a solid cord of energy all the way around the circle. Now feel that cord of energy begin to move clockwise around the circle. It begins slowly, but quickly picks up speed.

Feel the energy moving faster and faster around the circle. See it become like a solid ring of white light around the circle, moving through each person. Feel the energy as it moves through you.

Now imagine the energy building as it picks up still more speed. See it begin to spiral upward—just a little at first, then more. See it spiraling

higher and higher, narrowing as it grows, to form a cone: a cone of white light rising up from the circle, spiraling clockwise faster and faster. Feel it moving through you, feel its speed and strength.

See the cone spiral faster and faster, becoming brighter and stronger. Think about your goals: see them, imagine them fulfilled, place them into the energy of the ever-spiraling cone.

Faster and faster it goes, impregnated with our magical intent, focused toward our goals, almost ready! Almost ready!

Now see the cone rise up out of the circle! . . . See it rise upward, higher and higher, carrying our goals into manifestation.

It rises higher and higher, and then disappears in a flash of blinding white light. The process will be complete when the circle is opened, but indeed the goals are accomplished even now."

Chapter
IV

Samhain

In keeping with my resolution to deal with ritual theory rather than merely creating a handful of ritual scripts, I have varied the elements of ritual in this and subsequent sections. Our first two rituals, the new and full moon Esbats, both used formal Correllian openings. Now we will introduce you to other ideas. In this ritual, instead of using the elements to prepare the ritual space, we will be using smudging. Here we will cast the circle "hand to hand." The quarter calls and toast will also be different from the formal casting. This will be true in each subsequent section, where we will introduce differing ideas, and mix and match them. In this way you can get a feel for the many different ways in which these things can be done. Never feel that you must do everything only one way. Variety is an important ingredient in effective ritual.

Samhain is the festival of the spirits. It is common to decorate the ritual space in a way that reflects that. Often the color black is predominant, and Hallowe'en images of skulls, skeletons, or ghosts are sometimes used. Some people really get into the Hallowe'en aspect of the holiday, and their ritual space can become rather *Grand Guignol* before they're done. Others represent the holiday in different ways—for example, using photos of loved ones now in the spirit world and items that bring them to mind. Still others consider Samhain's position as the final harvest festival and decorate with late autumn crops like pumpkins, squash, and corn. Because Samhain is also the Wiccan liturgical new year, some people emphasize that fact by using "Happy New Year" decorations.

In decorating your Samhain ritual space, you should of course do what feels right to you. Again, variety is a virtue and you should never feel that you have to do what someone else has done. Make the space your own, and decorate it in a manner that will have meaning to you and the others present.

Samhain is considered an especially good time for divination, and it is not uncommon to include divination in the ritual or after the ritual. Assuming you have a feast after your ritual, you might want to set a place for the spirits at the table. Or you might want to hold a Silent Supper. This is an old ritual to honor the ancestors in which the supper is eaten in complete silence. Sometimes the dishes are served in reverse order, and people enter and leave the room walking backwards, to emphasize in a highly literal way that they are communing with the Otherside. There are so many possible things to do for Samhain that we could not begin to describe them all, but independent research on the subject will give you many good ideas. In putting together a ritual, just remember that the only people you need to think about pleasing are the people in attendance.

• • • •

Air

For this ritual we will cleanse the space by smudging. This can be done by you or any member of the group.

Light a charcoal beforehand, so that it is ready to use by the time you begin. Make sure the charcoal is in a heat-resistant censer that can be picked up and carried, with a chain or handle that will not get hot.

When it is time to begin, have the people assemble *outside* the ritual space. After the space is cleansed they will be brought in one at a time.

Place dried sage or a powdered incense such as sage, cedar, or sandalwood on the hot charcoal in the censer. Take the censer and walk tuathail around the ritual area: fan the smoke throughout the space, either by hand or by using a ceremonial fan. Imagine all negative energy being forced out of the area and see the area being filled with yellow-white light.

Once the space is cleansed, move deosil around the area. Continue to fan the smoke throughout the ritual space and, as you do so, imagine it filling with blue-white light. It might be good to say something like:

"I bless this space . . . I bless this space . . . I bless this space . . . "

Now begin to bring the people in. Cleanse each person individually. Hold the censer before them and fan the smoke over them. Fan the smoke all up and down the front of the person's body, then have them turn around and do the same to the back side of their body. As you do so, focus on the person being cleansed of all negative energy and imagine them suffused with light. Next, welcome the person and allow them to enter the circle. Repeat this process for each person until all have entered the circle.

We will now cast our circle. For this ritual we will cast the circle from "hand to hand." To do this, begin by turning to the person deosil to you. Take their hand and say something like:

"From hand to hand I cast this circle."

Or you might say:

"From heart to heart I cast this circle."

Or you might say:

"In perfect love and perfect trust I cast this circle."

Or however you prefer to do it.

Then this person will take the hand of the next person and repeat the same words. The next person will do the same thing, and so on around the circle until it returns to you and everyone is holding hands. Now say something like:

"Behold, we join together to cast this circle, that it may be a token of the bond of love between us. Imagine the energy running from hand to hand, person to person. See the energy as beautiful, clear white light filled with strength and love and power. See the energy grow and strengthen. See it begin to expand around us, the circle of energy moving out around us to fill our ritual space and make a barrier at its edges. See that barrier become a wall of clear, strong white light: a wall to contain and strengthen our energy as we work.

*Behold, we do cut apart a place
between the realms of humankind
and of the Mighty Ones: a circle
of art to focus and contain the
powers we shall raise herein! The
circle is cast! So mote it be!"*

All: *"So mote it be!"*

Now release hands and continue.

. . . .

Fire

We will invoke the quarters using animal imagery. Using animal guardians at the quarters is a very ancient idea and is especially good if you have a shamanic bent.

Begin in the east. Use the wand, sacred tool of fire, or if you prefer, use your fingers. Raise the wand, imagining as you do so that a column of pure white light is arising in the east, at the border of the circle. See the column as strong and pure and filled with energy. Say something like:

East

*"I do invoke you, O golden eagle
of the east! Power of air! The
beating of your wings raises
the winds of inspiration and
enlightenment! Share with us
your powers of conception and
delineation, that we may have*

*clarity of mind and thought. Join
us, be with us, guide and inspire
us in this our holy ritual! We
bid you hail and welcome."*

All: *"Hail and welcome!"*

Now move to the next quarter. Again raise the wand and imagine a column of pure white light arising in the quarter. Say something like:

South

*"I do invoke you, O red dragon
of the south! Power of fire! You
breathe forth the flames of passion
and manifestation! Share with
us your powers of creativity and
courage that our actions may
be confident and effective! Join
us, be with us, guide and inspire
us in this our holy ritual! We
bid you hail and welcome!"*

All: *"Hail and welcome!"*

Now move to the next quarter. Again raise the wand and imagine a column of pure white light arising in the quarter. Say something like:

West

*"I do invoke you, O blue dolphin
of the west! Power of water! From
your blowhole you spout waves
of sensitivity and compassion!
Share with us your powers of love
and empathy that our emotions
may be open and free-flowing!
Join us, be with us, guide and
inspire us in this our holy ritual!
We bid you hail and welcome!"*

All: *"Hail and welcome!"*

Now move to the next quarter. Again raise the wand and imagine a column of pure white light arising in the quarter. Say something like:

North

*"I do invoke you, O black bear
of the north! Power of earth!
You make your home in the
cave that resonates with wisdom
and understanding! Share with
us your powers of focus and
integration that we may be steady
and well grounded! Join us, be
with us, guide us and inspire
us in this our holy ritual!"*

All: *"Hail and welcome!"*

Now it is time to invoke Deity. Since Grand Sabbats are lunar ceremonies, the Goddess will be invoked first. In this case we shall invoke the Goddess not in any particular personal form, but in her archetype as Crone. You might choose to invoke Deity for this ritual through a personal form. As you will remember from your First Degree studies, personal forms of this archetype include Hekate, Morrighan, and Kali.

The priestess raises her arms to call upon the Goddess. She might say something like:

Priestess: *"Hail unto you, O Crone of
Endless Ages! Grandmother! Ancient
One! Mistress of Magic and the Night,
Lady of Dreams and Visions! Enchant-
ress, Queen of Spirits and of the Otherworld. On this night when the veil is
thinnest, this night when we are most
conscious of our mortality and of our
immortality, we call to you! Stygian
Lady, who holds the keys of life and
death, who transforms matter and who
comforts the soul! Come to us now! We
bid you hail and welcome!"*

All: *"Hail and welcome!"*

Now imagine the Goddess entering the circle; imagine it in any way that makes sense to you, perhaps by imagining the Goddess in human form, as a shower of glittering light, or as a ball or tower of light appearing in the circle.

Now let us invoke the God in his archetype as Sorcerer. As you will remember from your First Degree studies, personal forms of this archetype include Cernunnos, Odin, and Santa Claus.

The priest raises his arms to call upon the God. He might say something like:

Priest: *"We invoke you O Sorcerer, Lord of Dreams and Midnight! Psychopomp! Guardian of the Gates of Life and Death! Guide and Guardian of the Spirits! Horned Hunter of the Night, who leads the Wild Ride of Souls! On this dark night, when we reach out to those who have gone before, we call to you, Lord of Visions! Guide us on our journey as you guide those who travel between the worlds! We bid you hail and welcome!"*

All: *"Hail and welcome!"*

Now visualize the God entering the circle.

Finally, invoke the ancestors. You might say something like:

"O mighty ancestors, beloved ones who have gone before, we invoke you and ask you to join us and to bless us! Ancestors of the Correllian Tradition, priestesses and priests, mothers and uncles of the lineage, spiritual family that aids and supports us, lend us your inspiration and your love, your guidance and your aid this night, we pray. Beloved ones, we bid you hail and welcome!"

All: *"Hail and welcome!"*

• • • •

Spirit

Begin by discussing the nature of the Samhain festival. Like all Sabbats, Samhain has many aspects; what you talk about now depends upon where you wish to put your emphasis. As you gain experience, you will find new facets of this and other ceremonies, for they will become more and more personal to you. They will open to you as a flower to the dawn and share with you their deeper meanings. In discussing the nature of Samhain you might say something like:

"We come together this night to celebrate the great feast of Samhain, summer's end. Now begins the winter of the year,

when the world turns to cold and death, and we turn inward and contemplate our lives and goals. It is the involution of the year: a time for visions and introspection, a time for rest and rejuvenation of the world's energies. On this night of all nights, we honor those who have gone before, the beloved ancestors. They are always with us, for the bonds of love and loyalty are not severed by death but endure and even strengthen from life to life and between. But at this time we are most conscious of the ancestors and spirit guides who help and aid us through the year, and this night we especially honor them. Now, too, beneath the patronage of the Great Crone Goddess, the Arch Witch, we are conscious of the magic in our lives and our own ability to transform and renew, even as she transforms and renews through the cycle of death and incarnation. For some the veil is thin from birth, but on this night the veil is thinned for us and we are all more magical, more able to hear the messages of Spirit.

Let us make good use of this."

Proceed now to your act of power.

. . . .

Act of Power
Ancestor Circle

Samhain is the festival at which we honor the ancestors. Some groups make more of this aspect of the holiday than others, often depending upon the strength of the group members' relationships with their ancestors. Some Wiccans are very strongly connected to their ancestors and honor them daily, often receiving clairvoyant messages from them on a regular basis. Other Wiccans feel very disconnected from their ancestors. However, we all have people we love who are among the spirits, and at this time of year it always good to honor them.

For this act of power you will need one candle for each person present; small birthday candles or emergency candles are best. You will also need a place to put the candles after they are lit—a bowl of earth in which they can be stuck upright (a cast-iron cauldron or something similar) or lots of little candle holders.

Make a special ancestor altar. This can be a place set aside on the normal altar or a separate altar unto itself. The ancestor altar should have room for the candles, which will ultimately be placed here, as well as room for an offering. It can be nice to ask people to bring photos of their ancestors to place upon the altar as well,

53

or special tokens representing them. You should also have one larger candle on the ancestor altar.

Begin by passing out the small candles to all present. Now address the idea of ancestors. You might say something like:

"On this night of all nights, when the veil between the worlds is at its thinnest, we honor those who have gone on before: the beloved ancestors.

Ancestors are those who have shaped us and made us what we are. Some are physical ancestors, family members now crossed over; others are spiritual ancestors, people to whom we are not related by blood but through love, who have shaped us through their example and actions—they have made us what we are, and we honor our spiritual tie to them.

Think now of your ancestors: the people in spirit whom you wish to honor and with whom you wish to remain linked. They are here. They are always here, wherever we are—for in the Otherworld there is neither space nor time as we know it, and the spirits are not limited by either. Think of your particular ancestors. Imagine them here in this room, standing among us. See them clearly and hold them in your hearts as we proceed.*

Beloved ancestors, we address you. Honored ones, beloved and holy ones, we know that you are always with us. Sometimes we can hear your voices, sometimes we cannot. But we know you are here. We call upon you, and ask you to be with us. On this night set aside for you, we honor and remember you especially. Dear ones, accept from us this offering, in token of our love and our respect."

Next, light the large candle on the ancestor altar. Then make an offering to the ancestors, perhaps a libation of water or wine, and/or an offering of flour or cornmeal. As you offer each, hold it up and imagine a shower of light pouring into it, filling it with energy.

Now proceed. Tell the people what they need to do; you might put it this way:

"One by one we will approach the altar. When your turn comes, think of your ancestors and light your

candle in their honor, then place it in the receptacle and leave it to burn for them. Speak to them, address them with words or with your heart; they will know."

Go first, so that the others see. Light your candle. Address your ancestors, aloud or silently. Then place your candle in the cauldron, bowl of earth, or candle holder as the case may be. Then step to the side, progressing in a deosil fashion. The next person will follow, then the next. As each person lights their candle and moves on, the group will slowly progress around the circle clockwise until arriving back in their original positions.

Next, join hands and begin a chant. If you are so inclined, you can also dance as you chant. A good chant might be:

"Spirits! Beloved spirits! Loved ones who have gone before!

Parted from us! Yet still with us! Connected to us—forever more!

Though our soul lives many lifetimes —yet the bond of love endures!

For the veil could never dim the light of a soul as bright as yours!

Spirits! Beloved spirits! Loved ones who have gone before!

Parted from us! Yet still with us! Connected to us—forever more!

Samhain

Beloved ancestors, we pray that our offerings have found pleasure in your eyes, and that you will keep us always in your hearts, even as we keep you in ours. We think of you always and honor our connection to you throughout the year, but at this time of year we are all the more aware of you and all the more anxious to thank you for your contributions to our lives. Dearest ancestors, may the blessing be upon you! So mote it be!"

All: *"So mote it be!"*

Now continue with the ritual.

• • • •

Water

To many Pagans alcohol is considered sacred. There are a number of reasons for this, one of them being that intoxication can resemble an ecstatic trance. Another reason, as the alchemists observed, is that alcohol represents the union of the feminine (water/liquid) and masculine (fire) polarities by virtue of being a liquid that will burn. Our flaming chalice blessing for this ritual draws upon this idea.

Let the chalice be prepared with an alcoholic beverage such as brandy. The priestess or someone else suitable will hold the chalice and represent the Goddess. The priest or someone else suitable will hold a consecrated match, lighter, or candle.

The priestess will face the people and present the chalice, holding it aloft. She should say something like:

"Behold, the womb of creation! The cauldron of eternity! The circle of life and death that returns ever unto itself!"

Now the priest faces the people and holds up the consecrated lighting instrument. He should say something like:

"Behold, the phallus of the God! The axis of the planes! The line of time and space that moves ever forward!"

Next, priestess and priest face each other. The priestess continues along these lines:

"In the beginning was the Goddess and she was alone and without form in the void of chaos. Within

her were the seeds of all things that would come later, for hers was infinite potential. And alone with all possibility she dreamed, and wondered about what possibility could become. Dreams moved to plans and plans to action; and behold, from within herself she created the God."

And the priest might say:

"And the God burst forth from the Goddess with a Big Bang, an explosion of fire and light that shot out in all directions! This was the first creation, when God was split from Goddess: Son from Mother, Brother from Sister. And all that was motile, hot, and physical became the God. And all that was stable, cool, and ethereal remained in the Goddess. And the Goddess looked upon the God, and she desired him with exceeding desire."

Let the priestess continue:

"And the Goddess yearned to be one with God again. But she was told: 'To rise you must fall.' And so she separated the many souls

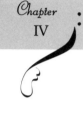

off from herself and sent them into matter, separate from her and yet always connected to her."

And now the priest:

"And thus did Goddess unite with God, and thus was the world formed as we know it. For each of us is both Goddess and God, soul and body, joined together in the mystery of life."

Next, the priest lights the match or lighter (a candle, if used, has already been lit) and places the flame in the fumes of the brandy, so that it is set alight.

This will be a very pale flame, delicate and blue, which will endure for a few minutes as it burns away the alcohol in the chalice. The priest and priestess continue thus:

Priestess: *"The God is not greater than the Goddess."*

Priest: *"Nor is the Goddess greater than the God."*

Priestess: *"But both are equal."*

Priest: *"And neither is complete without the other."*

Priestess: *"Therefore in the name of the Goddess . . ."*

Priest: *"And in the name of the God . . ."*

Together: *"May this chalice be blessed!"*

Both priestess and priest now flood the chalice with energy, seeing it filled with the bright, shining light of blessing.

Together: *"So mote it be!"*

All: *"So mote it be!"*

· · · ·
Earth

Now you will close the ceremony and open the circle.

Begin by giving thanks to the ancestors and the deities.

"Beloved ancestors, you who have gone before, your wisdom and your example guide us. We pray that you will be with us and aid us as we go forward, that we may call upon the strength and knowledge of the past, even as we build the future. We thank you for your presence and your aid this night and at all times. May you blessed be in all things. We

offer you our love and our respect!
We bid you hail and farewell!"

All: *"Hail and farewell!"*

Priestess: *"Beloved and Holy Crone Goddess, Mother of Mysteries, Lady of the Spirits, Queen of Darkness! From you we come, and to you we shall return! We thank you for your presence and your aid this night and at all times. We offer you our love and our respect! We bid you hail and farewell!"*

All: *"Hail and farewell!"*

Priest: *"O Sorcerer, Lord of Visions! Master of the Gate of Life and Death! Psychopomp and Guardian of the Spirits! We thank you for your presence and your aid this night and at all times. We offer you our love and our respect! We bid you hail and farewell!"*

All: *"Hail and farewell!"*

Now thank each quarter. Start in the north.

North

"We thank you, black bear of the north! Power of earth! We rejoice in the guidance and the

aid you give us! May the blessing be upon you now and always! With love and with respect we bid you hail and farewell!"

All: *"Hail and farewell!"*

Using the wand, pull down the tower of white light that was erected when the north was called.

Now turn to the west.

West

"We thank you, blue dolphin of the west! Power of water! We rejoice in the guidance and the aid you give us! May the blessing be upon you now and always! With love and with respect we bid you hail and farewell!"

All: *"Hail and farewell!"*

Using the wand, pull down the tower of white light that was erected when the west was called.

Now turn to the south.

South

"We thank you, red dragon of the south! Power of fire! We rejoice in the guidance and the aid you give us! May the blessing

be upon you now and always!
With love and with respect we
bid you hail and farewell!"

All: *"Hail and farewell!"*

Using the wand, pull down the tower of white light that was erected when the south was called.

Now turn to the east.

East

"We thank you, golden eagle
of the east! Power of air! We
rejoice in the guidance and the
aid you give us! May the blessing
be upon you now and always!
With love and with respect we
bid you hail and farewell!"

All: *"Hail and farewell!"*

Using the wand, pull down the tower of white light that was erected when the east was called.

Now you must open the circle. Begin in the east. Take up the athame and point it toward the eastern quarter. Devoke the circle, walking tuathail around it, imagining the barrier of light disappearing and returning back into the tip of the athame. Now speak the charm:

"Behold: As above, so below! As
the universe, so the soul! As within,
so without! May the circle be open
but never broken! Merry meet,
merry part, and merry meet again!"

Now have everyone cleanse and release all excess energy.

. . . .

Variations

Following are several other possible acts of power that you might use for a Samhain ceremony. It is our goal, as we have said, to give you some idea of the scope and variety that may be in ritual practice. Potential acts of power are innumerable, and creativity and reverence should guide you in building a wide repertoire to use in your own rituals. Variety in ritual is desirable—it helps to keep people interested and engaged; there are few worse flaws in ritual style than stagnation.

. . . .

Act of Power #2
Totentanz

Our second act of power for Samhain is a Totentanz, or Dance of Death. Also called *la danse macabre*, it is a theme arising from the late Middle Ages; here it is offered with a distinctly Pagan turn of thought.

The Totentanz takes its origin from a major artistic motif of the late Middle

Ages: the image of Death leading people of all social strata into the Otherworld in a kind of dance. This *Grand Guignol* image became prominent after the Black Plague had decimated the population of Europe. The image remains a potent one today, its most famous modern version being the Ingmar Bergman film *The Seventh Seal*.

For many people today the Totentanz is an unsettling, even horrifying image. But to the people of the times, overwhelmed by the reality of the plague, the Totentanz seems to have been rather reassuring, as it can be to the modern Pagan for whom death is not a fearsome ending but merely a spiritual transformation.

In the Totentanz we are reminded that all in their turn must die, and that death can and should be viewed as a natural part of life rather than as a terror to be avoided.

For this act of power you will need one person to portray Death. Costuming Death can be as simple as a skull-face mask or can be as creative as you like. If you prefer a less macabre Death, think in terms of the Horned God as guardian of the gate. But however simply or elaborately Death is costumed, Death must carry a cane, staff, or even a scythe to represent the Staff of Life and Death.

It can also be fun to have everyone wear costume for this ritual. Using the Totentanz as a theme, each person can dress as a representative of a different kind of person or as different professions. This can be very creative and entertaining for people.

For this enactment of the Totentanz, begin with everyone in a circle holding hands, except Death—who should be to one side of the altar. Have Death address the group. Death might say something along these lines:

• • • •

"Samhaintide is the season of death. The crops in the field have died, felled to feed the world in the hungry months to come. The leaves on the trees have turned color and are dying, too. The sun that once burned so brightly now sinks into the death of winter—shadows lengthening, days shortening. The liturgical year dies. We, too, must die in our turn. It is the nature of life.

Death is the great leveler. Whomever you may be—high priestess, elder, Paladin, rich, poor—it matters not. All in their turn must die. A rich banker, death will come. A loving mother, she too must die. A poor beggar—in death all are equal.

I carry the Staff of Life and Death. One touch of the staff ends life. A touch from the other end and a new life begins. All who are touched by my staff are transformed.

I am the guardian of the gate to the Otherworld. All must come through me, no matter who they are. Beyond the gate is happiness in the Land of Youth. Loved ones are reunited. Illness and pain are forgotten. Questions are answered. But first one must pass through Death."

. . . .

Begin a chant. An appropriate chant might be:

*"Nunc ubi Aradia,
multum mirabilis?*

*Aut ubi Ursula,
vox invincibilis?*

*Vel Caroline ubi est,
magistra nobilis?*

*Et ubi gloria nunc
—vita amabilis?"*

[*Where now is Aradia,
greatly miraculous?*

*Or where is Ursula, of
invincible voice?*

*Or Caroline where is
she, noble teacher?*

*And where your glory
now—beloved life?*]

As the group chants, Death dances tuathail around the circle. After going all

the way around the circle once, Death then begins randomly picking people out of the circle, tapping them on the shoulder with the staff. As each person is tapped, they stop singing and join Death, dancing with Death tuathail around the rest. Gradually the chanters dwindle, until at length only one person remains singing, all the rest of the people dancing tuathail behind Death in silence. Then Death takes the final person. Now all join hands in a circle with Death and continue silently dancing tuathail. After a few more times around, Death stops the dance and cries out something to the effect of:

*"Fall down! Fall down in
death and rest in peace!"*

Everyone—except Death—now sinks down to the floor, lies down, and closes their eyes. Death continues with a meditation. The meditation should not move so fast that people aren't able to keep up with it, but it shouldn't move too slow either. It might be done like this:

*"Go now within yourself! Deep
within yourself. Leave this moment
behind. Go deeper, deeper. See
yourself in a new place, a fair land.
Let the image come to you. Here all
is beauty and peace. Here are the
birds of Rhiannon, the messengers*

*of Spirit. Here are the beloved
ones, the ancestors. Here is the
Goddess, Mistress of the Feast.
Look around and you will see
her in the distance: the Goddess,
Queen of Spirits. Go to her. She
is the origin and destination of all
things. Give her greeting. How
does she appear to you? Hold out
your hands to her, for she has a gift
for you. Receive it from her . . .*

*Behold the gift you receive. What
is it? How does it make you feel?
Is there a message with it?*

*Accept the gift and give thanks
for it. Thank the Goddess for all
her gifts and for all she does for
you. O Fountainhead of Life. You
who were with us before birth and
who awaits us after death, we
thank you for the gift of life! We
thank you for all the opportunities
you afford us! Help us, we pray,
always to see the gifts of abundance
that are before us and to make
the most of the lessons each
precious life affords our soul!*

*Now take leave of the Goddess
and contemplate the gift you
have received from her . . . ”*

Give the people a few seconds to contemplate the gift that they have received
in meditation. Again, this should not last
too long, or people will become unfocused
and restive. After the ritual, if people wish
to discuss what they received in the vision,
you can help them to interpret what the
gifts mean, as the meaning is likely to be
symbolic in nature.

Then Death continues:

*“One touch of my staff brings
instant death. But a touch of the
other end of the staff brings rebirth!
All who are touched by the staff are
reborn—cleansed and rejuvenated
from their rest in the Otherworld!
Return then when you are touched
by the staff, filled with peace and
joy, invigorated and refreshed!”*

Death now moves deosil around the
circle, touching each person with the other
end of his staff. After touching them, Death
should then assist each person to stand, until one by one all are again standing.

*“Death is inescapable for all! But
death is not an end. Rebirth follows
death as surely as dawn follows*

night! As surely as spring follows winter! Death is a time to rest and to regroup before continuing on. Be joyful therefore and remember the words of Dryden: 'Death has no power the immortal soul to slay!'"

Now begin a sprightly chant and dance deosil around the circle in token of rebirth. A good chant might be:

"Unbroken circle of Forever
Starting always, ending never!
What a joyful happenstance
Is life and death's eternal dance."

Now continue with your ritual.

• • • •

Act of Power #3
Hekate Key Blessing

Hekate is the ancient Greek goddess of magic and Witchcraft. A moon goddess, Hekate had aspects as Maiden and Mother but was generally thought of as the Crone. For many, Hekate remains the consummate Crone and special patron of Samhain.

Also called Trivia, "The Triune," images of Hekate often have three heads or three bodies. The black dog was Hekate's animal form, and she is connected to Cerberus, the three-headed black dog who guarded the gates of the Otherworld in Greek mythology.

Hekate's symbols include the lighted torch, common to most Greek chthonic Gods, the ritual knife and the scourge, as well as the key. It is with this last symbol that this act of power deals.

The key is a very powerful symbol, as you may have already observed in these lessons. The key unlocks what is hidden, reveals mysteries. This is why we use the term *key* to describe symbolic forms that help us to shift our consciousness and work magic.

For this act of power you will need some keys. They can be real keys—elegant antique keys if you have access to them, prosaic modern keys if these are more accessible to you—or they can be images of keys: cardboard cut in the shape of a key, miniature keys made for charm bracelets, or the image of a key incised in clay. Make sure that you have enough keys for everyone who will be present. It is always better to have too many than too few.

Assemble your keys in a bowl or basket and place them on the altar before ritual begins.

Once you have cast your circle, invoked, and spoken of the holiday a bit, you can proceed to this act of power if you wish.

Take up the keys and speak about them. You might say something like this:

"A key . . . a skeleton key perhaps?
A little Samhain humor there.

*What is a key? The opener of
doors: The revealer of hidden
things. A key gives passage into
what has been barred, makes
a path through barriers.*

*We all have many barriers—things
we wish would move forward in our
lives but don't: Situations for which
we need answers or understanding,
which elude us. Paths that seem to
lead only to locked doors. Locked
doors for which we need a key . . .*

*The key is the symbol of the great
Crone Goddess, Mistress of Magic.
Magic can open many locked doors,
especially those that are within
us. She, our Goddess, can open
all doors, answer all questions. All
knowledge is hers, and therefore
also ours if we seek it through her.*

*Consider this, as we look upon
these keys. They are only tokens of
her power, 'keys' if you will, to help
us call upon her ability to open and
transform—symbols of a process we
invoke. But symbols, as you know,
are keys that help us understand*

*what the mind cannot always
understand through other means.*

*Therefore, as we bless these
keys let us think of our Lady in
her form as Crone and invoke
her transformative powers into
our lives through these humble
symbols of her wisdom."*

Next, lead everyone in a chant. If you
are so inclined, place the basket of keys
on the floor in the center of the circle and
dance around it while you chant. A good
chant might be:

*"Darksome Goddess, send a key
Blessed with Samhain energy!
Open my eyes that I might see
What answers may await for me!"*

Continue to chant and/or dance until
you feel the energy has built up enough.
Then stop and have everyone focus the energy into the keys. You might say:

*"Now let us focus the energy
we have raised into the keys.
Imagine the energy rushing into
the basket of keys, filling it with
light and power. See the energy
glowing within the basket—filling
each key, shining with strength*

and light. Imagine the basket of keys glowing as if it were a sun in the center of our circle, light radiating in all directions!

O Great Crone Goddess! Hekate! Pandeina! Queen of Night, Mother of Mysteries! You who guard all secrets and all hidden things, in your name may these keys be blessed! May they bring us the answers to our questions, the openings we seek in our lives! Holy Lady, Grandmother, aid us in this our undertaking, we pray! So mote it be!"

All: "So mote it be!"

Next, continue:

"Now take a moment to think about your life. Think of a situation or a question whose solution eludes you, a part of your life that seems blocked or closed to progress, which needs to be answered or opened up. A situation for which you need a key . . .

One by one, we will each take a key from the basket. As you take your

key, close your eyes and focus on the situation you have thought of, and ask the Crone to guide you."

Let each person take a key, moving deosil around the circle. When everyone else has taken theirs, then you should select yours. Tell the people:

"We will take our keys home tonight, after the ritual, and use them to bring us the unlocking of the situations on which we have focused. Carry your key with you, in your pocket or on a chain. Keep it under your bed at night, until your situation is resolved. Resolution will come soon."

Now continue with your ritual.

Chapter

V

Yule

Yule is the feast of Midwinter, and in decorating your ritual space for Yule you may want to emphasize evergreen wreaths and boughs, pinecones, and red and green candles. These are all very atmospheric for Yule. Don't forget that Santa Claus is a form of the Old God. Santa images can be appropriate, especially the more "wizardry" ones, with long robes and staves. You may wish to have a Yule tree, decorated with garlands, lights, and Pagan-themed ornaments. This ties in to very ancient themes.

Yule is the time of the rebirth of the sun, and solar images and themes are also very appropriate to Yule. White and gold is another common color theme for Yule, picking up on the solar aspect.

Have fun with Yule and take advantage of the Midwinter decorations easily available at this time of year. But as always, the most important thing is to make it meaningful and special to you and those who are with you.

Air

For this ritual we will cleanse the space with mineral salts and alcohol. To do this you will need some mineral salts of the sort used for making bath salts. These should be readily available in a craft store. Epsom salts also work well. You will also need rubbing alcohol. It is best to use the mineral salts in their natural state. You can sometimes successfully use bath salts depending on how they have been made, but they will not be as effective.

Have everyone already assembled.

Place the mineral salts in a fire-resistant container. A tinfoil container, such as those used for baking, is ideal, as the mineral salts will leave a residue that is hard to clean. Add alcohol to the mineral salts, enough to soak them well.

Now say something like:

"Behold, we shall join together to cleanse this space. Even as these salts burn, so too shall all negative energy in this space be transformed and transmuted, consecrated, and blessed. So too shall our own energy be cleansed and blessed as well. So mote it be!"

All: *"So mote it be!"*

Light the mineral salts using a match, candle, or consecrated lighter. They will set up a bright, pale, cleansing flame that will raise the vibration of the energy.

Allow the mineral salts to burn for a bit, and then lead the people in a visualization to internalize the effects. You might do it like this:

"Behold the flame, dancing before us. Feel the strength in it, the power. Feel its energy, moving and transforming all it touches— transmuting all negativity. Imagine the flame growing brighter, expanding, growing larger and larger. See the flame expand to fill the space between us, then expand beyond us. See it grow and expand farther and farther, until it fills our entire ritual space with transformative light. Feel the energy moving all around you. Feel the energy moving within you as well. Feel it raising your vibration, cleansing you, eliminating all negative energy. Even as the fire burns, the vibration rises. Negative energy is transformed and becomes positive. The circle is cleansed, and we are cleansed with it."

Allow the fire to burn until it goes out. Then say something like:

"Behold, it is done. So mote it be!"

All: *"So mote it be!"*

We will now cast our circle. For this ritual we will cast our circle using visualization. You will need to lead everyone in visualizing the creation of the circle, which might go something like this:

*"Let us join hands.
Become aware of your heart chakra.
Imagine a ball of clear white light
in your heart chakra: beautiful,
clear white light. And in that light
feel strength, love, and peace. Have
this image clear in your mind, feel
the energy strongly. Now let that
energy begin to move and expand
within you, filling your body. Let
the energy fill you, move within
you, filling and suffusing you
with beautiful, clear white light.*

*Now feel a bit of that energy
within you begin to move out from
you. See it begin to flow deosil
around the circle. Feel the energy
connect with the energy of the
other people present, forming a*

*circle of white light, moving from
hand to hand around the circle.
See the circle of white light moving
from person to person around
the circle, growing stronger and
brighter, moving faster and faster.*

*Let the circle begin to expand
beyond us. See it move out to the
edges of our ritual space. See the
circle expand and grow brighter and
stronger as it does so, moving deosil
around the ritual space, moving
faster and faster. See the white
light expand upward, forming a wall
or moving light around us, a battery
and a focusing barrier to strengthen
our working and increase its effect.
See this boundary clearly, feel its
energy, and the focusing effect it
has upon the energy of the circle.*

*Behold, we do cut apart a place
between the realms of humankind
and of the Mighty Ones: a circle
of art to focus and contain the
powers we shall raise herein! The
circle is cast! So mote it be!"*

All: *"So mote it be!"*

Now release hands and continue.

Fire

In this ritual we will invoke the quarters in terms of their astrological associations. The zodiac signs can be taken as representing the building blocks of human nature, and thus, as above so below, of all things, so by invoking them we especially stress the interrelation of all things that exist, and our connectedness to all things.

Begin in the east. Use a wand, sacred tool of fire, or if you prefer use your fingers. Raise the wand, imagining as you do so a column of pure white light arising in the east, at the border of the circle. See the column as strong and pure and filled with energy. Say something like:

East

"I invoke you, O ladies and lords east, powers of air and thought, and in your name I call forth the powers of your children: Gemini, Libra, Aquarius! Share with us their flexibility of mind and inspiration! Join us we pray and aid us in this our holy ritual! We bid you hail and welcome!"

All: *"Hail and welcome!"*

Now move to the next quarter. Again raise the wand and imagine a column of pure white light arising in the quarter. Say something like:

South

"I invoke you, O ladies and lords of the south, powers of fire and manifestation, and in your name I call forth the powers of your children: Aries, Leo, Sagittarius! Share with us their passion of spirit and courage! Join us we pray and aid us in this our holy ritual! We bid you hail and welcome!"

All: *"Hail and welcome!"*

Now move to the next quarter. Again raise the wand and imagine a column of pure white light arising in the quarter. Say something like:

West

"I invoke you, O ladies and lords of the west, powers of water and emotion, and in your name I call forth the powers of your children: Cancer, Scorpio, Pisces! Share with us their sensibility of heart and empathy! Join us, we pray, and aid us in this our holy ritual! We bid you hail and welcome!"

All: *"Hail and welcome!"*

Chapter V

Now move to the next quarter. Again raise the wand and imagine a column of pure white light arising in the quarter. Say something like:

North

"I invoke you, O ladies and lords
of the north, powers of earth
and integration, and in your
name I call forth the powers of
your children: Taurus, Virgo,
Capricorn! Share with us their
strength of constitution and
determination! Join us we pray
and aid us in this our holy ritual!
We bid you hail and welcome!"

All: "Hail and welcome!"

Now it is time to invoke Deity. Since the Lesser Sabbats are solar ceremonies, the God will be invoked first. In this case we shall invoke the God not in any particular personal form, but in his archetype as Sorcerer. You will remember that some personal forms of this archetype include Cernunnos, Secullos, Odin, and Santa Claus.

The priest raises his arms to call upon the God. He might say something like:

Priest: "We invoke you, O Sorcerer, Lord of
Midwinter! Giver of Gifts and Visions!
Horned One—Lord of the Otherworld
Feast! Now at this time of greatest
darkness, your power is ascendant and
the year's involution is deepest! You who
guard and protect the sleeping Earth,
who blankets the buried seeds—we call
to you and with love and with respect we
pray that you will join and aid us in this
our holy ritual! O Mighty Sorcerer, we
bid you hail and welcome!"

All: "Hail and welcome!"

Now imagine the God entering the circle. Imagine it in any way that makes sense to you, perhaps by imagining the God in human form or as a shower of glittering light or as a ball or tower of light appearing in the circle.

Now let us invoke the Goddess in her archetype as Crone. You will remember from First Degree studies that some personal forms of this archetype include Hekate, Morrighan, and Kali.

The priestess raises her arms to call upon the Goddess. She might say something like:

Priestess: "Grandmother Crone! Mistress
of Magic and Enchantment, Queen of
the Otherworld and Lady of the Spirits! Most Ancient One and Wisest!
You who engender the life that the God

protects. We call to you and invoke you! Be with us we pray and guide and aid us in this holy Yuletide ritual! As the Darkest Night passes and Light is reborn, your eternal Wheel turns once more! Grandmother, with love and with respect we bid you hail and welcome!"

All: *"Hail and welcome!"*

Now visualize the Goddess entering the circle.

Finally, invoke the ancestors. You might say something like:

"O mighty ancestors, beloved ones who have gone before, we invoke you and ask you to join us and to bless us! Ancestors of the Correllian Tradition, priestesses and priests, mothers and uncles of the lineage, spiritual family that aids and supports us. Lend us your inspiration and your love, your guidance and your aid this night, we pray. Beloved ones, we bid you hail and welcome!"

All: *"Hail and welcome!"*

• • • •
Spirit

Begin by discussing the nature of the Yule festival. Like all Sabbats Yule has many aspects you can talk about, depending upon where you wish to put your emphasis. What you may wish to emphasize is up to you. In discussing the nature of Yule, you might say something like:

"We come together to celebrate the festival of Yule, or Midwinter. At this time the powers of the Old God are at their height, the sun's light has ebbed to its lowest point, and the involution of the world is deepest. Tonight the Light is reborn. From this night forward the days will lengthen again, the sun grow stronger. The Young God begins to grow and the process of his return is set in motion, even while the Old God yet reigns. The Old God will continue to rule for a time and winter has far to go before it ends, but the cycle of renewal has begun."

• • • •
Act of Power
Gift Exchange

In selecting ideas for a Yule ritual, you should take advantage of the rich cultural and mythical traditions that surround this holiday.

One thing that you might wish to do for Yule is a gift exchange. This is a common practice both in secular and Pagan society.

Ask each person to bring a gift to exchange. It is wise to set a specific price range that everyone can easily meet so that the gifts are not unequal. If your group is good at arts and crafts, asking them to make the gifts themselves might be nice, but make sure to give plenty of notice if you want them to bring homemade gifts because the Yule season can be very hectic and doing such things at the last minute may be neither practical nor satisfying.

The gifts should be wrapped so that their contents cannot be easily guessed.

Place the gifts in the center of the circle, either as soon as people arrive or at the beginning of the ritual. You might set them directly on the floor or perhaps put them into a large bowl or cauldron (big plastic cauldrons sold at Samhaintide are perfect for this sort of thing), depending on their size.

Have everyone join hands.

Invoke a blessing upon the pile of gifts. You might say something like:

"Behold, we do bless these gifts,
that they may be a token of the
bond of love that is between

us all. May they be blessed
to bring to their receiver joy,
success, and abundance.

Imagine a ball of light in your
heart chakra. A ball of beautiful,
clear white light. See that ball
of light grow stronger, clearer,
larger. Let the ball of light
radiate strength and love and
peace throughout your heart.

And from that ball of light in your
heart chakra, send forth a beam
of light into the pile of gifts at the
center of the circle. Fill the gifts
with the light from your heart.

Now imagine the gifts beginning
to shine, with light glowing and
radiating with energy, and in that
energy is love and joy and strength
and peace. See the energy growing
stronger and stronger. Now we
will dance, and as we dance let us
continue to focus energy into the
gifts, and imagine the blessing
growing in strength and power."

Begin to dance in a clockwise circle around the gifts. As you dance, sing a seasonal chant. A good choice might be:

Yule

"Circle we the carol now!
Singing joyfully and how!
Tread the measure, smile and bow
In the Old God's honor!"

When you feel that you have danced and chanted enough, and the energy is strong, stop the dance and focus back upon the gift pile. Direct everyone to focus into the gifts the energy that has been raised. You might say:

"Imagine all of the energy that has
been raised being sucked into the
gifts, see it entering them and filling
them. Behold—may the blessing
be upon these gifts! So mote it be!"

All: *"So mote it be!"*

If your group is sufficiently athletic, you might choose to follow this by jumping the gift pile, similar to how we jump the fire at other times of year. If not, proceed directly to distribution.

Have everyone close their eyes and take a gift. It is important that people close their eyes and select randomly, since this confers a divinatory aspect to the proceedings; each person's gift can be interpreted as a prediction for the coming year.

You may choose to have people open their gift immediately and interpret in circle, or you may wait and do this after ritual

as part of the feast. Some examples of how gifts might be interpreted: A pen set might indicate that the recipient needs to do some writing—perhaps an article or a book, or a letter to a specific person. Incense might indicate an increased spirituality for the recipient, or you might interpret the incense by its specific type: cleansing, say, if lavender, or romance if rose or orange. A Yule ornament might indicate rejoicing for the recipient or perhaps another meaning depending upon its color and shape.

Like any omen, the meaning of each gift may vary with the person, so make sure everyone understands that what's important is what the gift means *to them*.

Now continue on with the ritual.

· · · ·

Water

For this ritual we are going to use a group blessing for the chalice. For obvious reasons this blessing is best with a small group.

Fill the chalice with the desired beverage. Then raise it up, and hold it in the center of the circle. Ask everyone present to place one hand upon the chalice and join you in blessing it. You might lead them in the blessing like this:

"Become aware of your heart
chakra. Imagine it filled with
clear white light, shining and

glowing with love and strength. In that light feel the love of Spirit, moving within you.

Now send energy from your heart chakra through your hand and into the chalice: energy filled with love, with joy, with creativity. Fill the chalice with energy. See the chalice filled with shining light, radiating out in all directions, growing stronger and stronger.

O Mother Goddess! O Father God! Beloved ones! Join us we pray in blessing this holy chalice! Lend your energy to ours! Bless this chalice with love and strength! May it be as a bond between us, a bond of enduring love. A bond between yourselves and all of us: a bond between ourselves and one another. Behold! May the blessing be!"

Now pass the chalice deosil around the circle, letting each person drink. You should go last and offer the final bit to Spirit.

Or if you prefer, you can pass out paper cups and fill them from the chalice, asking everyone to wait and drink together. Make sure to fill one cup for Spirit. If you do

this, you may wish to offer an appropriate toast, such as:

"To the Lady! To the Lord! To us!"

All: *"To the Lady! To the Lord! To us!"*

• • • •

Earth

Now you will close the ceremony and open the circle.

Begin by giving thanks to the ancestors and the deities.

"Beloved ancestors, you who have gone before, your wisdom and your example guide us. We pray that you will be with us and aid us as we go forward, that we may call upon the strength and knowledge of the past, even as we build the future. We thank you for your presence and your aid this night and at all times. May you blessed be in all things. We offer you our love and our respect! We bid you hail and farewell!"

All: *"Hail and farewell!"*

Priest: *"May thanks be given unto you, O Sorcerer, Lord of Midwinter. Though you yet rule, the light shall wax and* days grow longer! May the blessing be upon you now and always! We thank you for your presence and your aid this night and at all times. We offer you our love and our respect! We bid you hail and farewell!"

All: *"Hail and farewell!"*

Priestess: *"We thank you, O Crone, Queen of winter and of the Spirit Realm! Arch Witch, Mistress of Magic and of Visions! We thank you for your presence and your aid this night and at all times. We offer you our love and our respect! We bid you hail and farewell!"*

All: *"Hail and farewell!"*

Now thank each quarter. Start in the north.

North

"May thanks be given unto you, O ladies and lords of the north, powers of earth and integration! And may thanks be given unto the powers of your children: Taurus, Virgo, Capricorn! We thank you with love and with respect for your guidance and your aid in this our holy ritual! May there be

peace between us now and always! We bid you hail and farewell!"

All: *"Hail and farewell!"*

Using the wand, pull down the tower of white light that was erected when the north was called.

Now turn to the west.

West

"May thanks be given unto you, O ladies and lords of the west, powers of water and emotion! And may thanks be given unto the powers of your children: Cancer, Scorpio, Pisces! We thank you with love and with respect for your guidance and your aid in this, our holy ritual! May there be peace between us now and always! We bid you hail and farewell!"

All: *"Hail and farewell!"*

Using the wand, pull down the tower of white light that was erected when the west was called.

Now turn to the south.

South

"May thanks be given unto you, O ladies and lords of the south,

powers of fire and manifestation! And may thanks be given unto the powers of your children: Aries, Leo, Sagittarius! We thank you with love and with respect for your guidance and your aid in this our holy ritual! May there be peace between us now and always! We bid you hail and farewell!"

All: *"Hail and farewell!"*

Using the wand, pull down the tower of white light that was erected when the south was called.

Now turn to the east.

East

"May thanks be given unto you, O ladies and lords of the east, powers of air and thought! And may thanks be given unto the powers of your children: Gemini, Libra, Aquarius! We thank you with love and with respect for your guidance and your aid in this our holy ritual! May there be peace between us now and always! We bid you hail and farewell!"

All: *"Hail and farewell!"*

Using the wand, pull down the tower of white light that was erected when the east was called.

Now you must open the circle. Begin in the east. Take up the athame and point it toward the eastern quarter. Devoke the circle, walking tuathail around it, imagining the barrier of light disappearing, returning back into the tip of the athame. Now speak the charm:

"Behold: As above, so below! As the universe, so the soul! As within, so without! May the circle be open but never broken! Merry meet, merry part, and merry meet again!"

Now have everyone cleanse and release all excess energy.

• • • •

Act of Power #2
Candle Circle

Our second act of power is in the nature of a simple mystery play, followed by a candle circle. It should be noted that these can also be done separately. Change the wording for the candle circle, and it is also quite appropriate for Candlemas.

For the mystery play you will need three people: one to be the Oak King, one to be the Holly King, and one to be the Crone Goddess. For the candle circle you will need one candle for each person present, a lighter, and a fire-resistant bowl or cauldron.

The candles need not be elaborate; a package of birthday candles will do fine. You can also use the small white candles commonly sold for emergency use. Smaller candles are better for this because they need not burn long.

The play can be enacted very simply. It is permissible for the speakers to read their parts. Other than the candles, no props are necessary.

Of course it is more spectacular if the speakers can memorize their parts. And as you can imagine, it can be a lot of fun to costume the participants but this is not necessary.

Make sure that the person portraying the Crone Goddess already has the lighter and a candle, as all will be dark when these are needed.

Holly King: *"I am the Holly King, Lord of winter and of Night. I am the Kindly One. Under my rule the earth sleeps beneath a blanket of protective snow and rests in preparation for coming rebirth. I am the lord of wisdom, and of wealth. I am the Giver of Gifts and also the Giver of Visions. I am the Lord of the Gate, who guards the path between life and death and the magic realm between. I am Cernunnos. I am*

Merlin. I am Santa Claus. I am the Sorcerer. I am the God who fell with the harvest and rules in death, yet I am not dead; for death is an illusion and spirit but changes its form. I am not sad or woeful. I am the jolly God of Midwinter celebrations, the joyous God of the Otherworld Feast. Behold me, the Lord of Midnight, the slain sun, the Horned God of the Spirit realm, and know that life is never absent, even in death. With the deepest of sleep come the most vivid of dreams. Beneath the frozen earth, the hidden seeds wait for spring. Behind the veil of death, spirits await rebirth. When the night is darkest, then dawn is near. Just so, when all seems still, it is often that change is merely waiting for the right moment to happen."

Oak King: *"Indeed! I challenge you, O Lord of Death!"*

Now let the two kings engage in a mock struggle. The kings can grapple with each other or have a choreographed mock sword fight, or they could use quarter staves; do whatever works best for you. At length the Oak King vanquishes the Holly King, who falls to the floor.

Holly King: *"I am wounded! I am struck! In the midst of my greatest power I am cast down!"*

Oak King: *"It is even so. Now the longest night shall pass, the days will lengthen, and the sun will climb high in the heavens. For behold! I am the sun reborn! I am life renewed! I am the Oak King, and in my time I shall rule the longest day! I shall grow with the plants and crops, and renew the life of Earth. I shall arise with the ram and melt the snows of winter—for I am the heat that nurtures the seed and makes the blood run faster. I shall turn the Goddess's head to love, and all things will flower in my name. But that is yet to come. For now the Old King shall rule a little longer, but his end is begun. Days may grow colder for a time, but they will also grow longer and winter will pass away. All things in their turn are reborn: the day, the earth, the soul. For the only constant is change and spirit but changes its form. The longest night is the moment of the Holly King's greatest power but also the beginning of his end. Go now into the long night with him. What would you release with him as he passes away? What would you change*

as the days lengthen? Think of these things. Meditate upon them now, as we let the longest night come about us."

Let the Oak King now extinguish the altar lights so that the room is in complete darkness. Meditate upon all that you would change or release. Meditate for about a minute, maybe two. More will be too much if you have people who aren't skilled in meditation.

Now the Crone takes the lighter and lights her candle. The candle should be held under the face so that the Crone is eerily underlit. This will also provide light if the Crone's speech must be read.

Crone Goddess: *"Behold, I am the Crone, Queen of the Night, of winter and the Spirit Realm. I am old, immeasurably ancient. Bent and gnarled as the bare trees of winter, yet I am strong and sure of purpose. Even in this Darkest Night, I see clearly.*

Once I wore the red veil of the Maiden and danced among the flowers of spring. The world was my playground and I rejoiced. The sun's rays warmed me and moved me to love.

Once, too, I wore the white gown of the Mother and walked among the growing fields. The world was my child; I nurtured it and gave it sustenance. The sun was at my side, my partner and protector.

Now I wear the black mantle of the Crone and stand strong amidst the wind and snows of winter. The world is as one asleep, and I shelter it with my protective snows. The sun is my husband and I am now a widow.

I am the Queen of Witches. I have been all things and learned all secrets. I know that if we do not find that which we seek within, we can never find it without. I know too that perfection is a false goal, for it cannot exist. What is perceived as perfection is not an ending but a plateau that precedes new growth—no sooner is it reached than it must be moved beyond.

When the rose is at its most fragrant, it has already begun to rot. No sooner is the fruit ripe than it must fall. When the sun has reached its greatest height at noonday or at Midsummer, then it must begin to decrease. So, too, this longest night. From this point of greatest power, the reign of night shall diminish and the powers of the sun increase. The Old Lord will fade and be reborn as the Young Lord. All things shall be renewed.

It is even so in the affairs of human-kind. There is no greater surety than change and growth. The old must give way to the new; outmoded ideas and forms must be discarded that new and better ways may grow. It is the way of things.

In token of growth and renewal, let us now each light a candle.

As we light our candles, let us be mind-ful of the role of change in our lives. And let us consider the areas of our life where change and growth are needed. Even as the light increases, so too may we be re-newed and reborn."

The Crone now uses her candle to light the candle held by the person deosil to her. She may say something like:

"The light returns, may
you be renewed!"

That person will then use their candle to light the candle of the person deosil to them, saying:

"The light returns, may
you be renewed!"

And so forth deosil around the circle until each person's candle has been lit.

All: *"The light returns, we are renewed!"*

Now you may wish to sing an appropri-ate chant such as:

"The sun is renewed
The earth is renewed
All life is renewed
I am renewed!
Renewed!
Renewed!
Renewed!"

Collect all of the candles into your fire-resistant bowl. They may be left burning in the bowl or extinguished, if you prefer.

If you are so inclined, the still-burning candles in the bowl may be placed in the center of the circle and jumped over by each member; perhaps people might make a silent wish as they do so or shout out an affirmation such as *"Growth!"* Or if you are not up to such athletics, you may simply extinguish the candles, collect them in the fire-resistant bowl, and place them upon the altar.

Now continue with the rest of your ritual.

Of course it should be noted that the candle circle need not be done with the mystery play as shown; it can be done by itself or with any other prologue you prefer.

. . . .

Act of Power #3
Grail Procession

Our third act of power is an adaptation of the grail procession from the story of Peredur/Percival.

You may remember that in the story of Peredur the young knight comes to the castle of his uncle, the Grail King, who is crippled by a wound or illness. The Grail King is of course the Old God, the lame sun of winter, and his illness represents death.

That night, during a feast at the castle of the Grail King, Peredur witnesses a sacred procession. It is led by two men in polar colors who carry a long spear or sword between them. The spear or sword appears to drip blood from its tip. Behind a woman follows with a grail (a cauldron, not a chalice), in which is an image of a human head or skull. In some versions three women carry the grail, the Triple Goddess.

This is very ancient imagery. Peredur is asked what the procession means but does not answer. Later he is told that had he answered, the Grail King would have been restored to health.

Staging a version of this as part of the Yule ritual can be very moving.

Ideally, you will need two men dressed in polar colors: white and black, red and black, red and green, and so on. Between them they should carry an athame, sword, or spear, depending on availability. In a pinch, one man can carry the blade alone. You will also need a representation of a head or skull in a large bowl or cauldron. Again, the plastic cauldrons sold at Hallowe'en work very well. This will be carried by a woman.

Begin by having the men go to the altar and dip the tip of the blade into a vessel of red wine or grape juice, to represent blood. Then have the men with their blade and the woman with her grail process around the ritual area. You may wish to sing a chant as this is done. A good choice might be:

"A circle of Mystery—
a circle of might!
Deep as the galaxies—
a circle of night!
Holy and ancient—
the Mystery revealed!
If we can answer the Question
—then the King shall be healed!"

When the procession has finished, ask the group the sacred question, *"What are these things and who do they serve?"*

The answer, of course, is the most important part of the rite. Make sure that at least one person present can give the answer, as otherwise it is a very bad omen indeed, for reasons that are obvious.

The answer to the question is this: The spear/sword represents the God. It is the power of life, which is demonstrated by the blood/grape juice. It is linear in form, moving always forward. But it is born by polar powers, birth and death, which are the vehicles that move it forward. The grail represents the Goddess, who is the origin and inner essence of all things. It is the womb of creation. It is circular in form because it has neither beginning nor end and is separate from considerations of space and time. The head inside the cauldron represents the soul that is hidden in all things. The Celts, like many peoples, regarded the head as the seat of the soul. Thus we see that the physical proceeds from the spiritual, propelled by the cycle of birth and death, with the soul/Spirit at its center.

When the question has been answered, say something like:

"Behold! The Mystery is revealed!
The sun is healed and reborn!
From this night forward he shall
grow stronger again, and health
and joy shall return to the land!"

If you like, another chant and dance might follow here—something fast and joyful. A good chant might be:

"Return! Return! O sun, return!
Born of darkness, lord of light!

Return! Return! O sun, return!
From the middle of this darkest night!
Return! Return! Grow brighter still!
The days shall longer grow!
Return! Return! Grow brighter still!
For the dawn shall come
and darkness go!
Return! Return! O sun, return!
Born of darkness, lord of light!
Return! Return! O sun, return!
From the middle of this
darkest night!"

Then continue with the ritual.

· · · ·

Variation

If you do not have space for a full-fledged procession, a variation on this is to place the Epopteia, or sacred items, in a bowl or basket covered by a lid or veil. Uncover the basket and show it to all present, asking the sacred question, *"What are these things and who do they serve?"*

Another interesting variation to this act of power for the more theatrically inclined group is to have someone play the part of the Grail King. The Grail King's outer costume should make him appear old and ill, even mortally wounded. But when the question is answered, the Grail King can throw off his outer costume and emerge as

the reborn young sun king. Then he himself can declare his healing and rebirth.

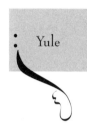

Yule

Chapter

VI

Imbolc

Imbolc is the festival of the Maiden Goddess, whose associations include the dawn and the inner fire. This Sabbat is regarded as the Dawn of the Year. For this reason, many traditions consider Imbolc an ideal time for initiations and other new beginnings.

For Wiccans, Imbolc is the Festival of Light. At Imbolc we celebrate and encourage the return of the sun, reborn at Midwinter. Days have begun to lengthen and, although in many places winter is still very much in evidence, the energies of spring are stirring. As a rule, you want to have as many candles for Imbolc as possible, since their flame represents the returning sun's energies.

The Imbolc Sabbat is often associated with the color white. In the Correll Mother Temple, Lady Krystel always set up the Imbolc altar with white altar cloths of lace and candle holders, offering bowls and chalice of glittering crystal. This created a very magical impression, which has never left me.

Some people like to make use of candle crowns, similar to those associated with Lucia Day in Europe. These consist of a number of lit candles rising from a crown of evergreen foliage and are meant to represent the activation of the crown chakra. These headdresses can be very exciting, but there is a technique to making them that is too long to go into here; if you are interested in trying it out, you can research how to make them.

Conversely, because it is also associated with the dawn, Imbolc decorations can also incorporate dawn's many colors: vivid golds, oranges, lavenders, and pinks. This gives a very different feel that can be quite nice.

Of course, one of the most famous customs associated with Imbolc is the groundhog oracle. Some temples like to enact this for themselves—using a hamster, guinea pig, or even a person. Others prefer to wait for the results of famous secular groundhogs such as Punxsutawney Phil or General Lee.

There are many interesting Imbolc customs you can research, but as always you want to use what makes sense to you and the people with you, and what helps your magical process.

. . . .
Air

For this ritual we will cleanse the circle by ceremonial sweeping. Make sure the broom that is used for this has been consecrated beforehand as a ritual tool. The type of broom does not matter; it may be of any type, from an ordinary household broom to a special ceremonial broom actually made from the broom plant.

When it is time to begin, have the people assemble *outside* the ritual space and wait while you cleanse the circle. After the space is cleansed, they will be brought in one at a time.

You or whoever is going to cleanse the area should begin by sweeping tuathail. Sweep the ritual area thoroughly in this manner. Concentrate on sending out all negative energy from the ritual space, and imagine the negative energy rushing out of the area. Imagine the area being filled with cleansing yellow-white light. It might be appropriate to say something like:

> *"I cleanse this space . . .*
> *I cleanse this space . . .*
> *I cleanse this space . . . "*

When the space has been cleansed, turn and begin to sweep deosil. Now focus on blessing the area and preparing it for the ritual. Imagine the ritual area filling with blue-white light. It might be desirable to say something like:

"I bless this space . . . I bless this space . . . I bless this space . . . "

Next, place the broom at the altar and bring the people in one at a time. Have the people wait at the boundary of the ritual space until their turn comes. Anoint each person with consecrated oil, using the oil to make the sign of the pentagram or the crescent moon on their forehead or on their wrist. Check beforehand to make sure that no one is allergic to scented oil. If anyone is allergic, use something else such as olive oil or consecrated water instead. Say something like:

*"May you be blessed in the
name of the Old Gods. In
perfect love and perfect trust
be welcomed to this circle."*

Then let the person enter and repeat the process with the next, until all have entered.

Now we will cast the circle. For this ritual we will cast the circle using a Shakespearean casting based upon an altered version of the "Black Spirits" passage of Shakespeare's Scottish play.

Begin in the east. Take up the athame and point it outward, visualizing a beam of white light shooting from the athame's tip to what will be the outer edge of the magic circle. Now begin to walk deosil around the circle, imagining the beam of light "drawing" a boundary of light around the circle's edge.

From the east, walk deosil around the circle, imagining a barrier of light being formed by the beam. Speak the charm:

*"Black spirits and red,
White spirits and gray,
Come ye! Come ye!
Come ye as come ye may!
Around, around, around about:
All good come in, all ill keep out!"*

As you walk, imagine the boundary growing brighter and stronger, becoming a wall of white light. As you come back around to the east, completing the circle, see the boundary become a solid circle of light around the ritual area. Make this as strong as you can.

The circle is now cast.

. . . .

Fire

In this ritual we will invoke the quarters through the forms of the Goddess. This can be particularly good for Grand (Lunar) Sabbats, moons, and other rituals that honor the feminine polarity.

Begin in the east. Use a wand, sacred tool of fire, or if you prefer, use your fingers. Raise the wand, imagining as you do so a column of pure white light arising in the east, at the border of the circle. See the column as strong and pure and filled with energy. Say something like:

East

"We call upon you, O Red Lady of the East! You who took the first action and in so doing set the world in motion. Lady of the Dawn, and of all beginnings! Behold, we do invoke you O Lady of the East and with you the sylphs and spirits of the air! Come to us! Join us! Lend us your aid and your inspiration in this our undertaking!"

Now move to the next quarter. Again raise the wand, and imagine a column of pure white light arising in the quarter. Say something like:

South

"We call upon you, O White Lady of the South! You who united with the God and ensouled the world! Lady of noonday, mistress of fertility and of fecundity! Behold, we do invoke you, O Lady of the South, and with you the salamanders and spirits of the fire! Come to us! Join with us! Lend

us your aid and your inspiration in this our undertaking!"

Now move to the next quarter. Again raise the wand and imagine a column of pure white light arising in the quarter. Say something like:

West

"We call upon you, O Gray Lady of the West! You who govern the cycles of time and rebirth. Lady of sunset, who gathers home the fruits of creation! Behold, we do invoke you, O Lady of the West, and with you the undines and spirits of the waters! Come to us! Join us! Lend us your aid and your inspiration in this our undertaking!"

Now move to the next quarter. Again raise the wand and imagine a column of pure white light arising in the quarter. Say something like:

North

"We call upon you, O Black Lady of the North! You who were before the first creation and who shall endure beyond all reckoning. Lady of Midnight, you who are the darkness before the dawn. Behold, we do invoke you, O Lady of the North,

and with you the gnomes and
spirits of the earth! Come to us!
Join us! Lend us your aid and your
inspiration in this our undertaking!"

Let the four quarters now be portrayed by four people. Since we are invoking the quarters as forms of the Goddess, it is likely that these will be four women; however, this need not be viewed as a requirement. A man may embody the divine feminine just as a woman may embody the divine masculine, since both polarities are present in all things. The four people may be costumed for the parts or not as desired. Most commonly you would have had these same four people invoke the quarters as well as personifying them in the dance that follows, but this, too, need not be a requirement. If you do not have four people to do this, then you should omit the physical dance and use only the spoken parts with one or two people taking all the parts.

Have the four quarters now come to the center of the circle and join hands. Let them dance deosil in the center of the circle singing an appropriate chant, such as:

"Air! Fire! Water! Earth!
Air! Fire! Water! Earth!
Air! Fire! Water! Earth!
We are one!

We are one!
We are one!"

Now speak the charm:

"Behold: four queens dance,
and by their dance the world is
formed! As it was in the beginning
the dance of the elements sets
the ritual in motion! Thought!
Action! Reaction! Integration!
An endless cycle of being!

"Behold the dance and imagine the
energy raised by its steps! See the
energy arising between the dancers,
shining white and radiating in
all directions. See that light grow
and expand. See it moving out
beyond the dancers, expanding
to encompass them, surround
them, then expanding still farther!
See the light fill our ritual space,
growing brighter and brighter,
expanding farther and farther until
it surrounds the entire ritual space.
See the light form a barrier all the
way around us, a barrier of light. A
circle of art to focus and to contain
the powers we shall raise herein!

"Behold! By our will so mote it be!"

Imbolc

89

All: *"So mote it be!"*

Now it is time to invoke Deity. Since Grand Sabbats are lunar ceremonies, the Goddess will be invoked first. In this case, we shall invoke the Goddess not in any particular personal form but in her archetype as Maiden. You will remember from First Degree studies that some personal forms of this archetype include Athena, Hathor, and Erzulie.

The priestess raises her arms to call upon the Goddess. She might say something like:

Priestess: *"Hail unto you, O Maiden! We do invoke you, Dawn—Mistress, Lady of Renewal and Rebirth! Your many colors herald the return of the sun, and you share them generously with the newborn flowers that shall emerge with spring. Mistress of the rainbow and of all arts and forms of creation—we bid you hail and welcome!"*

All: *"Hail and welcome!"*

Now imagine the Goddess entering the circle. Imagine it in any way that makes sense to you, perhaps by imagining the Goddess in human form or as a shower of glittering light, or as a ball or tower of light appearing in the circle.

Now let us invoke the God in his archetype as Hero. You will remember from First Degree studies that some personal forms of this archetype include Apollo, Mars, and Thor.

The priest raises his arms to call upon the God. He might say something like:

Priest: *"We invoke you, O God, in your form as Hero! Gentle Lord of the Rising Sun, of Spring and New Beginnings! Eromenos! Lord of love and beauty, passion and creativity! Your fire, reborn, only just begins to burn in this holy season, yet we welcome the flame! We bid you hail and welcome!"*

All: *"Hail and welcome!"*

Now visualize the God entering the circle.

Finally, invoke the ancestors. You might say something like:

"O mighty ancestors, beloved ones who have gone before, we invoke you and ask you to join us and to bless us! Ancestors of the Correllian Tradition, priestesses and priests, mothers and uncles of the lineage, spiritual family that aids and supports us, lend us your inspiration and your love,

your guidance and your aid this
night, we pray. Beloved ones,
we bid you hail and welcome!"

All: *"Hail and welcome!"*

. . . .

Spirit

Begin by discussing the nature of the Imbolc festival. Like all Sabbats, Imbolc has many aspects and what you emphasize is up to you. In discussing the nature of Imbolc, you might say something like:

"We come together to celebrate the
festival of Imbolc, or Candlemas.
This is the Feast of Light, when
we celebrate the returning light of
the slowly waxing sun. In some
places spring has arrived, and in
others we pray for spring to come
soon. New life has begun to emerge
from beneath the shroud of winter
and the earth has already begun
to be renewed. This is the time of
the Maiden, the lady of light and
color who rules the dawn and the
spring. It is a time of growth and
creativity, of rebirth and renewal.
Let us therefore, like the newborn
leaves and first spring flowers,
strive to open and unfold, taking

this time to begin to shake off
the deep involution of winter."

. . . .

Act of Power
Fire Lighting

Our act of power for Candlemas centers on the idea of fire lighting. In this it is very similar to the candle circle from our Yule section, which is also appropriate for Candlemas with some modification.

The idea of striking a new fire and using it to relight previously extinguished lights is an ancient ceremony of rebirth and renewal that is almost universal. For many ancient peoples, it was a ceremonial act of supreme importance. Here we have combined the idea with the idea of the Eternal Flame, also an ancient idea and one that is central to Correllian thought and the focal point of our Wiccaning ceremony.

For this act of power you will need lots of candles. As well as many altar candles, you should have a candle for each person present.

Have all of your candles assembled on the altar. Begin the ritual with only one single candle lit at the center of the altar. This will be termed the Spirit candle. By this solitary light, cast the circle, invoke, and speak about Candlemas a bit. Then you are ready for your act of power. You might lead into it like this:

Imbolc

"Now is the Dawn of the Year. The Darkest Night—Yule—is past. Life begins to stir and will soon return to the world. But we know that it always seems darkest before the dawn. The coldest part of winter falls between Yule and the return of spring, and although the days have grown longer, they are not yet warmer. Indeed, though the Darkest Night is past, it is still the Dark of the Year and still we turn inward awaiting the return of warmth and green.

It is now, in the coldest time, that we most ardently pray for the return of the sun. Now when we raise our energy to help him to reawaken and restore the earth to fruitfulness. Now that we think of the first creation, when the Goddess, trembling, beheld the God whom she had created from herself and desired him, even as the earth beholds the sun and desires his embrace to bring on the spring."

Hold up the Spirit candle. Continue along these lines:

"Now is the time of the Maiden, the Dawn of the Year when all things are possible. Now we consider our potential, for the year lies waiting yet undiscovered, even as the earth, unfurrowed, awaits the planting season. What will grow? What we will plant? Whatever we wish. All is beginning. All is potential.

To the Maiden all things are possible, as it was in the beginning when the Goddess had only just taken the first step of creation and all paths awaited to be trod. All is excitement at such a moment, for possibility is limitless. As she beheld the God, as she beheld the flicker of manifestation, she knew what could be. That anything could be. Let us never forget that feeling; we carry it within us all for at our core we were there. We were within her even as she is within us now. All things are possible; we can create, we can form our will through the physical plane. Remember . . .

Let this one flame remind you. One flame, burning in the darkness, alone and without equal.

So it is with Spirit. One flame,
immeasurably ancient yet always
new. One flame from which all
other flames are lit, reflected in
their myriad lesser flames.

One flame, an Eternal Flame,
which burns in all of us, which
lights our hearts and informs
our being. In token of this,
let us each take a candle."

Pass out the candles to everyone present. Then continue:

"One flame. One Spirit. One spark
of life. But one became two."

Begin now to light the altar candles. Use the Spirit candle to light them. Continue speaking:

"Two became more. More became
many. Many became myriad.
Myriad became exponential.

Even so did the Goddess send
the many souls into matter,
and the world was made.

Potential became manifestation.
Possibility became life.
Dreams put on form."

Now hold out the Spirit candle to the person nearest you, moving deosil. Address them:

"Light now your candle."

Let the person light their candle from the Spirit candle. Now move on from person to person deosil around the circle, allowing each to light their candle as you continue speaking:

"May this flame serve as a token
of another flame, a brighter flame,
an Eternal Flame that burns
within us all. May it remind us
that we are all manifestations
of Deity, and that because we
are manifestations of Deity all
things are possible to us, always.

Candlemas is the Dawn of the
Year, and for this year all hopes
are possible. Yet every instant we
exist is also a dawn, the dawn
of a new moment of creation,
for we create in every moment
we exist. Some of our creations
we are conscious of, some of our
creations we are not conscious of,
but conscious or unconscious we
create. Let us strive to be conscious
creators, responsible in our creation

Imbolc

and rejoicing in our handiwork,
even as she whose greater light
we embody and express."

When everyone has lit their candle, return to the altar.

"Even as the Goddess has made
her one flame into many, even
as we have brought our temple
from darkness to light, so too
shall the sun's light grow. Days
will grow longer and warmer,
the earth will reawaken, spring
shall come to the world and the
plants shall bud and flower. The
Goddess will adorn herself and
welcome the God's return. Let us
too welcome the return of life!"

Now continue with your ritual.

. . . .

Water

For our toast in this ritual you will need two people to represent the Goddess and the God. You will also need two beverages. The person representing the Goddess should have a dark beverage such as a red grape juice. The person representing the God should have a light beverage such as a white grape juice. The chalice will be held between them.

The Goddess should go first. Let the person representing the Goddess raise up the dark beverage and say something like:

"In the beginning was the Goddess.
And she was alone and without
form in the void of chaos before
the first creation. But she longed
to create, to work her will and give
form to existence. And the Goddess
dreamed and the Goddess planned
and the Goddess longed and from
her longing came the first creation.

In the name of the Goddess may
the blessing be upon this juice!"

Let the person representing the Goddess now bless the dark juice, filling it with light and energy.

Now let the person representing the God hold up the light beverage and say something like:

"And from the Goddess was
created the God. The Goddess
divided herself, sending all of the
fiery, active, physical aspects of
herself into the God and retaining
all of the watery, malleable,
spiritual aspects for herself.
And the God exploded out from
the Goddess in the explosion of

the first creation, sending fire
and light in all directions.

In the name of the God may the
blessing be upon this juice!"

Now let the person representing the
God bless the light juice, filling it with energy and light.

Then the person representing the Goddess continues:

"In time the light of the God
cooled and took form, becoming
suns and planets and asteroids.
The universe took shape and the
Goddess was pleased. She desired
to be part of this universe, to
rejoin with the God and be one
with him. But he fled from her as
the mouse flees before the cat."

Now the person representing the God:

"And she took counsel of her
Highest Self, which told her that
'To rise you must fall.' And so
the Goddess created the many
souls and sent them into matter,
so that through them she could
unite with the God. And so was
the world we know created."

Now let them fill the chalice together,
so that the dark juice and the light juice
are mingled.

Now pronounce a final blessing upon
the chalice:

"In the name of the Goddess and
of the God may this chalice be
blessed, that it may be a token
of the bond of love that exists
between ourselves and them, and
between them and all of creation!"

Let the person representing the Goddess draw up energy from the earth to bless
the chalice in the name of the Goddess.
Simultaneously, the person representing the God draws down energy from the
heavens to bless the chalice in the name of
the God. As they meet in the middle, finish the blessing:

"So mote it be!"

All: "So mote it be!"

Now pass the chalice deosil around the
circle, letting each person drink in their
turn. You should go last and offer the final
bit to Spirit.

Or if you prefer, you can pass out paper
cups and fill them from the chalice, asking everyone to wait and drink at the same
time. Make sure to have a cup for Spirit. If

you do it this way you may wish to offer a toast such as:

"To the Goddess! To the God! To us!"

All: *"To the Goddess! To the God! To us!"*

. . . .
Earth

Next, you will close the ceremony and open the circle.

Begin by giving thanks to the ancestors and the deities.

"Beloved ancestors, you who have gone before, your wisdom and your example guide us. We pray that you will be with us and aid us as we go forward, that we may call upon the strength and knowledge of the past, even as we build the future. We thank you for your presence and your aid this night and at all times. May you blessed be in all things. We offer you our love and our respect! We bid you hail and farewell!"

All: *"Hail and farewell!"*

Priestess: *"Beautiful Maiden! Joyful and courageous! We thank you for your presence and your aid this night and at all times. We offer you our love and our respect! We bid you hail and farewell!"*

All: *"Hail and farewell!"*

Priest: *"O Hero God, Lord of Rebirth! We thank you for your presence and your aid this night and at all times. We offer you our love and our respect! We bid you hail and farewell!"*

All: *"Hail and farewell!"*

Now thank each quarter. Start in the north.

North

"Black Lady of the North! We thank you for your presence and your aid in this holy ritual, you and the gnomes and spirits of the earth! May there be peace between us now and always! We bid you hail and farewell!"

All: *"Hail and farewell!"*

Using the wand, pull down the tower of white light that was erected when the north was called.

Now turn to the west.

West

"Gray Lady of the West! We thank you for your presence and your aid in this holy ritual, you and the undines and spirits of the waters! May there be peace between us now and always! We bid you hail and farewell!"

All: *"Hail and farewell!"*

Using the wand, pull down the tower of white light that was erected when the west was called.

Now turn to the south.

South

"White Lady of the South! We thank you for your presence and your aid in this holy ritual, you and the salamanders and spirits of the fire! May there be peace between us now and always! We bid you hail and farewell!"

All: *"Hail and farewell!"*

Using the wand, pull down the tower of white light that was erected when the south was called.

Now turn to the east.

East

"Red Lady of the East! We thank you for your presence and your aid in this holy ritual, you and the sylphs and spirits of the air! May there be peace between us now and always! We bid you hail and farewell!"

All: *"Hail and farewell!"*

Using the wand, pull down the tower of white light that was erected when the east was called.

Now you must open the circle. Begin in the east. Take up the athame and point it toward the eastern quarter. Devoke the circle: walking tuathail around it, imagining the barrier of light disappearing, returning back into the tip of the athame. Now speak the charm:

"Behold: As above, so below! As the universe, so the soul! As within, so without! May the circle be open but never broken! Merry meet, merry part and merry meet again!"

Now have everyone cleanse and release all excess energy.

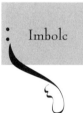

Imbolc

Act of Power #2

Blessing of the Quarters

Our second act of power for Imbolc is a blessing that makes use of the four quarters, and all they represent, to bless the returning sun. This act of power can stand on its own, or it can be used in conjunction with another, such as the fire lighting rite above.

For this act of power you will need four candles in the colors associated with the four quarters. You might also want to have a ceremonial fan, or a single feather, a feather fan of Native American inspiration, an Asian folding fan, or whatever you might like. The fanning can also simply be done with the hand. You will also want one candle for Spirit.

The people who called the quarters earlier in the ritual will enact this act of power, or if you prefer you might select different people to honor the quarters here.

Have the Spirit candle on the altar, along with the four candles for the quarters and the ceremonial fan, if you are going to use one.

Begin by explaining the idea. You might do it like this:

"At this time of year the sun is growing stronger, returning to the earth. Some years he comes slowly, others more quickly. Always we hope he comes quickly. The Maiden Goddess has opened the door of dawn, and awaits his return. She has called him. She longs for him. The earth awaits the warming touch of the light, the seeds sleep beneath the soil waiting for him to summon them to new life. All is in readiness for the sun's return.

In ancient times and still today, people would encourage the sun to return faster and do ritual to strengthen him and hasten the spring. That is what we are going to do tonight. In this ritual we are going to call the sun and bless the sun through the four quarters. Through this we will not only encourage the sun's return but strengthen the sun with the qualities of the quarters that will manifest in the coming months, and in our own lives as well."

Address the Maiden Goddess. You might say:

"Holy Maiden Goddess, Lady of the Dawn, Many-colored Mistress of the Arts. Inspire us in this our rite. You call the sun. You fling open the

Chapter VI

98

doors of the dawn and await his coming. You fill the sky with color to guide his way. We add our voices to yours. With you, we shall call the sun. We and all your children shall join you as you call. Through the four quarters and the twelve signs we shall connect with all things, and all shall call together with you, O Holy Lady. Inspire us and share with us the love you bear for him! In your honor, we light this candle."

Now light your Spirit candle. The other candles shall be lit from it, signifying the power of the Maiden Goddess.

Let the person who called the east during invocation come forward now and take up the quarter candle for the east. Let them light the candle of the east from the Spirit candle. Then let them turn to the east and raise the east candle in salute. They should take up the fan and fan the energy of the candle toward the east as they speak. Next, they should give a blessing, saying something like:

"In the name of the east, I call the sun! In the name of the east, I call the spring. In the name of the east, I call the God. May the God come and behold the Goddess in her freshness. Gemini!

Libra! Aquarius! Children of the east, arise and call the sun and bless him! May the God be blessed with the clarity and inspiration of the east! May we too be blessed! So mote it be!"

All: *"So mote it be!"*

Now let them set the east candle at the east quarter of the circle, and then return to their place.

The person who called the south during invocation now comes forward. Let them take up the quarter candle for the south. This person lights the candle of the south from the Spirit candle. Then they turn to the south and raise the south candle in salute. Let them take up the fan and fan the energy of the candle toward the south as they speak. Next, they give a blessing, saying something like:

"In the name of the south, I call the sun! In the name of the south, I call the spring. In the name of the south, I call the God. May the God come and embrace the Goddess in her beauty. Aries! Leo! Sagittarius! Children of the south, arise and call the sun and bless him! May the God be blessed with the courage

and passion of the south! May we too be blessed! So mote it be!"

All: *"So mote it be!"*

Now they should set the south candle at the south quarter of the circle, and then return to their place.

Let the person who called the west during invocation now come forward, taking up the quarter candle for the west. Let them light the candle of the west from the Spirit candle. Then this person should turn to the west and raise the west candle in salute. Let them take up the fan and fan the energy of the candle toward the west as they speak. Let them now give a blessing, saying something like:

"In the name of the west, I call the sun! In the name of the west, I call the spring. In the name of the west, I call the God. May the God come and love the Goddess in her fruitfulness. Cancer! Scorpio! Pisces! Children of the west, arise and call the sun and bless him! May the God be blessed with the love and compassion of the west! May we too be blessed! So mote it be!"

All: *"So mote it be!"*

Now let them set the west candle at the west quarter of the circle, and then return to their place.

Let the person who called the north during invocation now come forward. Let them take up the quarter candle for the north. Let them light the candle of the north from the Spirit candle. Then let them turn to the north and raise the north candle in salute. Let them take up the fan and fan the energy of the candle toward the north as they speak. Let them now give a blessing, saying something like:

"In the name of the north, I call the sun! In the name of the north, I call the spring. In the name of the north, I call the God. May the God come and support the Goddess in her power. Taurus! Virgo! Capricorn! Children of the north, arise and call the sun and bless him! May the God be blessed with the steadiness and wisdom of the north! May we too be blessed! So mote it be!"

All: *"So mote it be!"*

Now let them set the north candle at the north quarter of the circle and then return to their place.

Have everyone join hands.

"Behold, we have called the sun. We have called the spring. From the four quarters we have called him, and he shall come to join the Maiden Goddess. They shall rejoice in one another. The days shall continue to lengthen, the sun shall continue to brighten, the plants shall bloom and bud. Life returns to the world. So too shall our lives bloom. Let us think about the things we might like to see in these coming months. What are our goals? What are our wishes? Think on these and reflect upon them. Choose one that you particularly want. Let us ask the sun to bring it with him.

Behold, may these things we desire come into being, taking shape even as the sun grows stronger. As the sun waxes, so too may our goals strengthen and manifest. Divine Goddess, Divine God, we ask you to lend your power and aid us in this. Even as our Lord the sun grows strong, so too may our goals come into being. So mote it be!"

All: *"So mote it be!"*

Continue along these lines:

"Concentrate on this now. Imagine the sun growing stronger and our goals growing with him. See them coming into reality, taking shape and being accomplished. See them completed and accomplished, already ours, just waiting to manifest. Imagine this as we chant."

Begin a chant, and if space and inclination allow, dance deosil around the circle. A good chant might be:

"East! South! West! North! "Return, sun! Return! Air! Fire! Water! Earth! Return, sun! Return! Spring! Summer! Fall! Winter! Return, sun! Return! Return! Return! Return!"

Now focus the energy:

"Return, sun, return! May light and life return to the world! The Maiden awaits the spring; the earth awaits its awakening. We too await the season of light. May you grow, O sun. May we grow with you! May the earth be reborn

Imbolc

*and may our lives be renewed with
her. As the light waxes, we wax
as well! Return, sun, return!*

*Let us focus the energy. Imagine
it as a vortex of light in the center
of our circle. See the light shining
with strength and power, spinning
in the center of the circle, growing
brighter and brighter, faster and
faster! Imagine the light filled with
love and joy. Focus on your goals
and all that you wish to accomplish,
even as the sun grows strong and
the earth grows warm, and the
plants grow and flower. So, too,
may these things come to pass!*

*Now let us release our
energy—see it rising up, up,
up, and now—release!
And it is done—so mote it be!"*

All: *"So mote it be!"*

Now continue with the ritual.

• • • •

Act of Power #3
Rainbow Chakra Blessing

The Maiden Goddess is associated with
self-expression, creativity, and color. She
is the Goddess of the many-colored dawn,

of the variegated flowers that come with
spring, and of the rainbow. In this act of
power we will make use of the symbolism
of the rainbow and its connection to the
seven chakras and the seven planes.

For this act of power you will need seven
candles, in the seven colors associated with
the seven major chakras: red, orange, yellow,
green, light blue, dark blue, and purple. Arrange them in a row or in a circle on an altar
at the center of the ritual space. Or if you
are so motivated, you might obtain one of
the seven-color candelabras that are available in some metaphysical shops, which arch
like the rainbow and hold votive candles.

As each candle is lit during the ceremony, a blessing will be given. It is nice if
each of the seven blessings can be given by
a different person, but this is by no means
necessary. In fact, they can all be done by
one person if need be, but it is best to share
them so that more people take an active
role. The more people who take an active
role in ritual, the more emotionally successful the ritual is apt to be.

You will want to begin by discussing the
concepts involved. You might say something like:

*"Candlemas is the feast of light.
Now light is returning to the
world. The Maiden Goddess is
the Goddess of light—the light of*

the waxing moon, the light of the dawn. The light of the rainbow. The rainbow reveals the spectrum of light, its parts and qualities. As the rainbow symbolically corresponds to the divine archetypes, revealing the parts and qualities of Deity, so too the rainbow corresponds to the seven planes, revealing the parts and qualities of existence. So too the rainbow corresponds to the seven chakras, revealing the parts and qualities of the body's major energy centers. Through the rainbow a range of blessings are given. Tonight we honor the Maiden and her rainbow also."

You will also want to explain the mechanics. You might put it this way:

"During this rite we will invoke the powers of the rainbow and its correspondences, attuning to them and receiving their blessings. This ritual calls for a chant, in which all will join after each blessing. The words are simple: 'Blessed be the Holy Ones! Seven powers born in light. Blessed is as blessed does. Blessed be this holy night!' Now let us begin."

Now let the red candle be lit and a blessing said. After the blessing all will join in a chant. As the candle is lit, the person lighting it should envision it surrounded by a ball of clear white light and focus on this as they give the blessing. The blessing might be along these lines:

Red: *"Mine is the red flame of Saturn, the Crone. I bless this assemblage with vitality and practicality. May you always have the resources and support you need in life. May you learn your lessons and teach in your turn".*

All: *"Blessed be the Holy Ones! Seven powers born in light. Blessed is as blessed does. Blessed be this holy night!"*

Now let the orange candle be lit and a blessing said. As the candle is lit, the person lighting it should envision it surrounded by a ball of clear white light and focus on this as they give the blessing. The blessing could go something like this:

Orange: *"Mine is the orange flame of Mars, the Hero. I bless this assemblage with creativity and passion. May you always have joy and excitement in life. May you receive pleasure and give pleasure in your turn."*

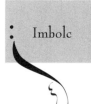

Imbolc

All: *"Blessed be the Holy Ones! Seven powers born in light. Blessed is as blessed does. Blessed be this holy night!"*

Now let the yellow candle be lit and a blessing said. As the candle is lit, the person lighting it should envision it surrounded by a ball of clear white light and focus on this as they give the blessing. The blessing would be to this effect:

Yellow: *"Mine is the yellow flame of Sun, the Lover. I bless this assemblage with courage and self-assurance. May you always have confidence and integrity in life. May you be encouraged and encourage others in your turn."*

All: *"Blessed be the Holy Ones! Seven powers born in light. Blessed is as blessed does. Blessed be this holy night!"*

Now let the green candle be lit and a blessing said. As the candle is lit, the person lighting it should envision it surrounded by a ball of clear white light and focus on this as they give the blessing. The blessing might be in terms like these:

Green: *"Mine is the green flame of Venus, the Maiden. I bless this assemblage with love and healing. May you always have balance and harmony in life. May you be loved and love in your turn."*

All: *"Blessed be the Holy Ones! Seven powers born in light. Blessed is as blessed does. Blessed be this holy night!"*

Now let the light blue candle be lit and a blessing said. As the candle is lit, the person lighting it should envision it surrounded by a ball of clear white light and focus on this as they give the blessing. The blessing should be along these lines:

Light blue: *"Mine is the light blue flame of Mercury, the Sorcerer. I bless this assemblage with intelligence and willpower. May you always have clarity and focus in life. May you gain knowledge and share it in your turn."*

All: *"Blessed be the Holy Ones! Seven powers born in light. Blessed is as blessed does. Blessed be this holy night!"*

Now let the dark blue candle be lit and a blessing said. As the candle is lit, the person lighting it should envision it surrounded by a ball of clear white light and focus on this as they give the blessing. The blessing might be to this effect:

Dark blue: *"Mine is the dark blue flame of Moon, the Mother. I bless this assemblage with psychic perception and magical ability. May you always be guided by and connected to your Higher Self* in life. May you receive many blessings and give blessings in your turn."

All: *"Blessed be the Holy Ones! Seven powers born in light. Blessed is as blessed does. Blessed be this holy night!"*

Now let the purple candle be lit and a blessing said. As the candle is lit, the person lighting it should envision it surrounded by a ball of clear white light and focus on this as they give the blessing. The blessing would go something like this:

Purple: *"Mine is the purple flame of Jupiter, the King. I bless this assemblage with spiritual understanding and wisdom. May you always know Goddess and see her hand in your life. May you have enlightenment and guide others in your turn."*

All: *"Blessed be the Holy Ones! Seven powers born in light. Blessed is as blessed does. Blessed be this holy night!"*

Now join hands around the candles on their altar. You might say something like this:

"Behold the rainbow—the seven colors of creation. Remember their blessings and consider how these might affect you in your

life. Imagine the energy of these blessings as a ball of clear, white light surrounding the candles. See that light grow brighter and stronger. As we chant, focus energy into that light, that these blessings may be amplified and multiplied."

Continue the chant; if space and inclination allow, you may wish to dance as well. Imagine the energy growing as you do so.

"Blessed be the Holy Ones! Seven powers born in light!

Blessed is as blessed does. Blessed be this holy night!

Blessed be the Holy Ones! Seven powers born in light!

Blessed is as blessed does. Blessed be this holy night!

Blessed be the Holy Ones! Seven powers born in light!

Blessed is as blessed does. Blessed be this holy night!

Blessed be! Blessed be! Blessed be!"

Now focus and release the energy. You might do it like this:

"Imagine that ball of energy
growing brighter and brighter,
stronger and stronger, shining
out in all directions like a sun in
the center of our circle—and let
us see that ball of light rise up,
up, up—higher and higher, see
the energy rise up and prepare to
release it . . . now! And see the
energy going out into manifestation
in a flash of brilliant light!"

Now continue with your ritual.

Chapter
VII

Ostara

Ostara is the festival of spring, and as a rule people incorporate spring themes into their decorations.

The vivid colors of the dawn are often used at Ostara—they show up in many-colored flowers, dyed eggs, and colorful altar cloths. Flowers, all kinds of foliage, and the image of the Green Man are also common elements in Ostara decor, as are images of baby animals. In recent years the idea of Ostara trees, decorated with colored eggs, has become popular in some circles.

Because Ostara once coincided with the sun's apparent entry into Aries, the ram is still a symbol associated with the holiday, as is the image of the Young God as shepherd. To the Romans this feast was known as Palilia and was especially associated with shepherds and with the shepherd god Pales. Fire jumping was one aspect of the Palilia, as it was among more northerly

Europeans as well, and it is still associated with the holiday today.

Of course Ostara is the vernal equinox, and the theme of perfect balance between light and dark is also quite appropriate. Themes in polar colors such as black and white, black and red, or red and white are very fitting.

Remember, too, that in some Wiccan traditions Ostara rather than Samhain is the beginning of the liturgical year, and so new year themes can be adopted as well.

As always, choose what works for you.

. . . .

Air

Begin by clearing and releasing all excess energy, as usual. Release all tensions and anxieties. Just let them flow through and out of your body, like a gentle wave of energy exiting through the soles of your feet.

Begin by cleansing the salt. Make three tuathail circles above it while visualizing yellow-white light. Imagine the light forcing out all negative or unfocused energy from the salt. Speak words to the effect of:

"Behold, I exorcise you, O creature of earth, casting out from you any impurities that may lie within."

The salt is then blessed: make three deosil circles above it, while visualizing blue-white light. Speak words to the effect of:

"And I do bless and charge you to this work!"

Next, cleanse the water, making three tuathail circles above it while visualizing yellow-white light forcing out all negative energy. Speak words to the effect of:

"Behold, I exorcise you, O creature of water, casting out from you any impurities that may lie within."

Then bless the water, making three deosil circles above it and visualizing blue-white light. Speak words to the effect of:

"And I do bless and charge you to this work!"

Address the salt, saying:

"Behold, the salt is pure!"

Then address the water, saying:

"Behold, the water is pure!"

Now take three pinches of salt and add it to the water, saying something like this:

*"Purity into purity then,
and purity be blessed!"*

Taking the mixed salt and water, walk deosil around the ritual space, aspersing the area while doing so. Visualize yellow-white light filling the area and forcing out all negative or unfocused energy. Say something like:

*"I cleanse you . . . I cleanse
you . . . I cleanse you . . . "*

When finished aspersing, return the salt and water to the altar.

Now turn to the token of fire. This will usually be either a lit charcoal or a book of matches (refer back to the First Degree lessons for other possibilities).

Cleanse the charcoal (or matches), making three tuathail circles above it with your hand while visualizing yellow-white light. Imagine the light forcing out all negative or unfocused energy from the charcoal, and then speak words to the effect of:

*"Behold, I exorcise you, O creature
of fire, casting out from you any
impurities that may lie within."*

Bless the charcoal, making three deosil circles above it with your hand while visualizing blue-white light. Then speak words to the effect of:

*"And I do bless and charge
you to this work!"*

Then turn to the token of air, usually either powdered or solid incense.

Cleanse the incense, making three tuathail circles above it with your hand while visualizing yellow-white light forcing out all negative energy. Speak words to the effect of:

*"Behold, I exorcise you, O creature
of air, casting out from you any
impurities that may lie within."*

Then bless the incense, making three deosil circles above it with your hand while visualizing blue-white light. Speak words to the effect of:

Ostara

*"And I do bless and charge
you to this work!"*

Now address the charcoal (or matches), saying:

"Behold, the fire is pure!"
Then address the incense, saying:

"Behold, the air is pure!"

Now take three pinches of powdered incense and sprinkle it onto the charcoal (or light the solid incense with a match), saying something like:

*"Purity into purity then,
and purity be blessed!"*

Take the burning incense and walk deosil around the ritual space, censing the area as you go. As you do this you should visualize blue-white light filling the area and charging its energy. As you cense the area, you may wish to say something like:

*"I charge you . . . I charge
you . . . I charge you . . . "*

Now we will cast the circle. For this ritual we will cast our circle using visualization. You will need to lead everyone in visualizing the creation of the circle, which might go something like this:

*"Let us join hands.
Become aware of your heart chakra.
Imagine a ball of clear white light
in your heart chakra—beautiful,
clear white light. And in that light
feel strength and love and peace.
Have this image clear in your mind,
feel the energy strongly. Now let
that energy begin to move and
expand within you, filling your
body. Let the energy fill you, move
within you, filling and suffusing you
with beautiful, clear white light.*

*Now feel a bit of that energy
within you begin to move out from
you. See it begin to flow deosil
around the circle. Feel the energy
connect with the energy of the
other people present, forming a
circle of white light, moving from
hand to hand around the circle.
See the circle of white light moving
from person to person around
the circle, growing stronger and
brighter, moving faster and faster.*

*Let the circle begin to expand
beyond us. See it move out to the
edges of our ritual space. See the
circle expand and grow brighter and
stronger as it does so, moving deosil
around the ritual space, moving
faster and faster. See the white
light expand upward, forming a wall
of moving light around us, a battery
and a focusing barrier to strengthen
our working and increase its effect.
See this boundary clearly, feel its
energy, and the focusing effect it
has upon the energy of the circle.*

*Behold, we do cut apart a place
between the realms of humankind
and of the Mighty Ones: a circle*

of art to focus and contain the
powers we shall raise herein! The
circle is cast! So mote it be!"

All: *"So mote it be!"*

Now release hands and continue.

. . . .
Fire

The quarters are now called, beginning in the east.

The priestess first asperses the quarter with the salt and water, visualizing the area suffused with yellow-white light. She says something like:

Priestess: *"By the powers of earth and water, I do cleanse and purify the quarter of the east."*

The priest then censes the quarter with the burning incense, visualizing the area suffused with blue-white light. He says:

Priest: *"By the powers of fire and air do I charge the quarter of the east."*

Begin in the east. Use a wand, sacred tool of fire, or if you prefer, use your fingers. Raise the wand, imagining as you do so a column of pure white light arising in the east at the border of the circle. See the column as strong and pure and filled with energy. Say something like:

East

"Hail unto you, O guardians of the Watchtower of the East, powers of air and inspiration! We invoke you, and ask you to be with us this night, to share with us your love, your guidance, and your inspiration. We pray that you will help us to open our minds and our eyes, and strengthen our thoughts as we go forward this night. We bid you hail and welcome!"

All: *"Hail and welcome!"*

Now move to the next quarter and repeat this process: aspersing, censing, and using the wand to draw up the pillar of light. Say something like:

South

"Hail unto you, O guardians of the Watchtower of the South, powers of fire and manifestation! We invoke you and ask you to be with us this night, to share with us your love, your guidance, and your inspiration. We pray that you will help us to open our courage and passion, and strengthen our resolve as we go forward this night. We bid you hail and welcome!"

Ostara

All: *"Hail and welcome!"*

Now move to the next quarter and repeat this process: aspersing, censing, and using the wand to draw up the pillar of light. Say something like:

West

"Hail unto you, O guardians of the Watchtower of the West, powers of water and compassion! We invoke you and ask you to be with us this night, to share with us your love, your guidance, and your inspiration. We pray that you will help us to open our hearts and our emotions, and strengthen our sensitivity as we go forward this night. We bid you hail and welcome!"

All: *"Hail and welcome!"*

Now move to the next quarter and repeat this process: aspersing, censing, and using the wand to draw up the pillar of light. Say something like:

North

"Hail unto you, O guardians of the Watchtower of the North, powers of earth and integration! We invoke you, and ask you to be with us this night, to share

with us your love, your guidance, and your inspiration. We pray that you will help us to open our souls and our Higher Selves, and strengthen our understanding as we go forward this night. We bid you hail and welcome!"

All: *"Hail and welcome!"*

Now it is time to invoke Deity. Since the Lesser Sabbats are solar ceremonies, the God will be invoked first. In this case we shall invoke the God not in any particular personal form, but in his archetype as Hero. You will remember from First Degree studies that some personal forms of this archetype include Apollo, Mars, and Thor.

The priest raises his arms to call upon the God. He might say something like:

Priest: *"Hail unto you, O God! We do invoke you in your form as Hero, Lord of the Rising Sun and of the Waxing Year! Master of Rebirth and New Beginnings! Trailblazer, who forges ahead where others fear to go! Lead us with you into the future! The Doors of the House of Dawn are opened and spring is upon us—let us move forward and embrace it! O Hero, with love and with respect we do bid you hail and welcome!"*

All: *"Hail and welcome!"*

Now imagine the God entering the circle—imagine it in any way that makes sense to you, perhaps by imagining the God in human form, as a shower of glittering light, or as a ball or tower of light appearing in the circle.

Now let us invoke the Goddess in her archetype as Maiden. You will remember from First Degree studies that some personal forms of this archetype include Athena, Hathor, and Erzulie.

The priestess raises her arms to call upon the Goddess. She might say something like:

Priestess: *"Wise and beautiful Maiden Goddess, we do invoke you! Goddess of creativity, beauty, and all arts, Guide and Guardian of heroes, we pray that you will join us and guide us in our holy rite. Even as you guided the heroes of old we pray that you will guide us to fully embrace all of our potential, even as now you guide the earth to rebirth and renewal! We bid you hail and welcome!"*

All: *"Hail and welcome!"*

Now visualize the Goddess entering the circle.

Finally, invoke the ancestors. You might say something like:

"O, mighty ancestors, beloved ones who have gone before, we invoke you and ask you to join us and to bless us! Ancestors of the Correllian Tradition, priestesses and priests, mothers and uncles of the lineage, spiritual family that aids and supports us, lend us your inspiration and your love, your guidance and your aid this night, we pray. Beloved ones, we bid you hail and welcome!"

All: *"Hail and welcome!"*

• • • •

Spirit

Begin by discussing the nature of the Ostara festival. Ostara, like all Sabbats, has many aspects you can talk about, depending upon where you wish to put your emphasis. In discussing the nature of Ostara, you might say something like:

"We come together to celebrate the festival of Ostara, to celebrate spring and renewed life. The reborn sun God rises as hero and the earth welcomes him. The return of the sun warms the earth and brings

Ostara

113

forth the living things—leaves and flowers open, spreading color and scent to delight the senses. The animals rejoice and become active; many bring forth their young. It is a time of new beginnings and of limitless potential. Rejoice then and embrace the spirit of life that moves in the world afresh! Let us, like hero and Maiden, walk where we have not walked before, embrace the new, and brave the unknown! Let us grow and expand even as light and life grow and expand at this time of year!"

. . . .

Act of Power
Egg Divination

Ostara is the festival of the spring, and its themes have to do with rebirth and new growth. It is an excellent time to be thinking of new directions or new projects for the coming summer.

Like many Pagan holidays, the customs of Ostara are shared to some extent with non-Pagans. An example is the use of symbols such as baby animals and eggs to represent rebirth. Flowers and the vivid colors of the spring are also associated with this holiday. Colored eggs have been used at the spring equinox for untold generations.

Our first Ostara act of power makes use of just these symbols.

For this act of power you will need a bowl of colored eggs. Use as many colors as possible. Place the bowl of eggs on the altar. When you have cast your circle and invoked, spoken of the nature of the Sabbat, and come at last to the body of your ritual, take up the bowl of eggs from the altar and hold it up so that all may see. Hold the bowl of eggs before you in the center of the circle, or pass it hand to hand. Speak about the symbolism of eggs. You might say something like:

"Behold, our friend the egg. From the most ancient times the egg has represented new beginnings, new life, new potentials yet unopened. New life is hidden within, but all that we see is the blank face of the shell. To celebrate Ostara we color eggs with all the colors of the dawn, to honor the Young Lord who is now reborn and the Maiden Goddess who has prepared the way for his coming, even as the many-colored dawn prepares the way for the sun.

Our lives, too, are a source of endless potential. Each dawn brings

in a new day, but who knows what
each day will hold? So it is with us;
as we enter this season of growth,
we come with many hopes, but
who can say what shall follow?

Think now on the coming
months of spring and summer.
What do you hope for? What do
you plan? Reflect on these."

Allow a few moments for reflection. When you feel that people have reflected long enough, begin a chant. A good choice might be:

"Powers of eternity
I know you abide in me
So by my will let me see
What the future holds for me!"

You might wish to place the eggs in the center of the circle and dance and chant around them. If you do not wish to dance, you will still want to hold or place the eggs in the center of the circle where all can focus on them. In either event, when the chant is finished have everyone focus energy into the bowl of eggs. You might direct them to do so like this:

"Imagine the bowl of eggs filling
with energy—see them glowing,
shining brightly with energy. Send

energy into the eggs, more, and
more . . . Behold, in the name
of the God and of the Goddess,
may these eggs be blessed to
our purpose! So mote it be!"

All: *"So mote it be!"*

Now take up the eggs again. Say something like:

"So many hopes and dreams. Who
can say how they shall befall?
Deity can. The Wise can. We
can. Take now an egg and close
your eyes and draw at random
that she may tell us what the
Dawn of the Year brings for us."

Have each person close their eyes and choose one egg. Then go around the circle and interpret each person's egg according to its color (or you can wait and do this after ritual if you prefer). For example, pink might mean love; blue, communication; lavender, spiritual growth; green, prosperity; and so forth.

Have each person hold on to their egg or set it in a safe place. Now continue with your ritual.

You might think it would be a good idea to combine this with the toast, so that the eggs are eaten in circle. We advise against doing so, however, as peeling boiled eggs

Ostara

is a messy business and time-consuming. Better to save the eating of the eggs for the feast after ritual.

. . . .

Variation #1

An obvious variation on this is to write a divinatory meaning directly upon the egg. Doing so allows you more leeway with your meanings, since they need not be tied to the colors of the eggs. Use a wax pencil or the special marking pens sold for egg decorating to write the meanings on the shell.

. . . .

Variation #2

Another variation is to buy the hollow plastic eggs that are commercially available in the spring. Inside of each hollow egg place an item such as a tumbled stone or a token of some sort that the recipient can take home after the ritual. Use all the same items on the inside and interpret the eggs by their color, or use different stones or other tokens on the inside and interpret by them, or write divinatory meanings on slips of paper and place inside the hollow eggs and divine from these, rather like fortune cookies.

. . . .

Variation #3

Our final variation on this simple act of power is to use flowers instead of eggs.

Get flowers of many colors and interpret the flowers according to color, just as you would the eggs. Or if you are familiar with the properties of flowers, you might get a selection of different types of flowers and interpret according to the type. For example, a rose might mean love. Obviously you would vary the spoken parts to allow for the qualities of flowers rather than of eggs, but the symbolism is very close.

. . . .

Water

We will now bless and share the chalice.

Here we will again use the flaming chalice blessing, which symbolizes the union of opposites by joining liquid with fire.

Let the chalice be prepared with an alcoholic beverage such as brandy. The priestess or someone else suitable will hold the chalice and represent the Goddess. The priest or someone else suitable will hold a consecrated match, lighter, or candle.

The priestess will face the people and present the chalice, holding it aloft. She should say something like:

Priestess: *"Behold the womb of creation! The cauldron of eternity! The circle of life and death that returns ever unto itself!"*

Chapter
VII

Now let the priest face the people and hold up the consecrated lighting instrument. Let him say something like:

Priest: *"Behold the phallus of the God! The axis of the planes! The line of time and space that moves ever forward!"*

Now priestess and priest face each other. The priestess continues along these lines:

Priestess: *"In the beginning was the Goddess and she was alone and without form in the void of chaos. Within her were the seeds of all things that would come later, for hers was infinite potential. And alone with all possibility, she dreamed and wondered about what possibility could become: dreams moved to plans and plans to action, and behold from within herself she created the God."*

And the priest might say:

Priest: *"And the God burst forth from the Goddess with a Big Bang, an explosion of fire and light that shot out in all directions! This was the first creation, when God was split from Goddess, Son from Mother, Brother from Sister. And all that was motile, hot, and physical became the God; and all that was stable, cool, and ethereal remained in*

the Goddess. And the Goddess looked upon the God and she desired him with exceeding desire."

Let the priestess continue:

Priestess: *"And the Goddess yearned to be one with God again. But she was told: 'To rise you must fall.' And so she separated the many souls off from herself and sent them into matter—separate from her and yet always connected to her."*

And now the priest:

Priest: *"And thus did Goddess unite with God, and thus was the world formed as we know it. For each of us is both Goddess and God, soul and body, joined together in the mystery of life."*

Ostara

Now let the priest light the match or lighter, and place the flame in the fumes of the brandy, so that it is set alight. Be very careful with this.

This will be a very pale flame, delicate and blue, which will endure for a few minutes as it burns away the alcohol in the chalice. Let the priest and priestess continue thus:

Priestess: *"The God is not greater than the Goddess."*

Priest: *"Nor is the Goddess greater than the God."*

Priestess: *"But both are equal."*

Priest: *"And neither is complete without the other."*

Priestess: *"Therefore in the name of the Goddess . . . "*

Priest: *"And in the name of the God . . . "*

Together: *"May this chalice be blessed!"*

Let both priestess and priest now flood the chalice with energy, seeing it filled with the bright, shining light of blessing.

Together: *"So mote it be!"*

All: *"So mote it be!"*

Now make certain that the flame is out. It does not take long to burn itself out, but it may be wise to cover the chalice for a few moments to make sure it is extinguished. Again, do be careful with this.

Now pass the chalice deosil around the circle, letting each person drink in their turn. You should go last and offer the final bit to Spirit.

Or if you prefer, you can pass out paper cups and fill them from the chalice, asking everyone to wait and drink at the same

time. Make sure to have a cup for Spirit. If you do it this way, you may wish to offer a toast such as:

"To the Goddess! To the God! To us!"

All: *"To the Goddess! To the God! To us!"*

. . . .

Earth

Now you will close the ceremony and open the circle.

Begin by giving thanks to the ancestors and the deities.

"Beloved ancestors, you who have gone before, your wisdom and your example guide us. We pray that you will be with us and aid us as we go forward, that we may call upon the strength and knowledge of the past, even as we build the future. We thank you for your presence and your aid this night and at all times. May you blessed be in all things. We offer you our love and our respect! We bid you hail and farewell!"

All: *"Hail and farewell!"*

Priest: *"O Hero God, Lord of Youth and New Beginnings! Master of the Dawn! We thank you for your presence and your aid this night and at all times. We offer you our love and our respect! We bid you hail and farewell!"*

All: *"Hail and farewell!"*

Priestess: *"O gracious Maiden Goddess, Rosy-fingered Harbinger of Light and Life! We thank you for your presence and your aid this night and at all times. We offer you our love and our respect! We bid you hail and farewell!"*

All: *"Hail and farewell!"*

Now thank each quarter. Start in the north.

North

"Hail unto you, O guardians of the Watchtower of the North, powers of earth and integration! We thank you for your presence here this night. May there be peace between us, now and always. Stay if you will, go if you must. We bid you hail and farewell!"

All: *"Hail and farewell!"*

Using the wand, pull down the tower of white light that was erected when the north was called.

Now turn to the west.

West

"Hail unto you, O guardians of the Watchtower of the West, powers of water and compassion! We thank you for your presence here this night. May there be peace between us, now and always. Stay if you will, go if you must. We bid you hail and farewell!"

All: *"Hail and farewell!"*

Ostara

Using the wand, pull down the tower of white light that was erected when the west was called.

Now turn to the south.

South

"Hail unto you, O guardians of the Watchtower of the South, powers of fire and manifestation! We thank you for your presence here this night. May there be peace between us, now and always. Stay if you will, go if you must. We bid you hail and farewell!"

All: *"Hail and farewell!"*

Using the wand, pull down the tower of white light that was erected when the south was called.

Now turn to the east.

East

"Hail unto you, O guardians
of the Watchtower of the East,
powers of air and inspiration! We
thank you for your presence here
this night. May there be peace
between us, now and always.
Stay if you will, go if you must.
We bid you hail and farewell!"

All: "Hail and farewell!"

Using the wand, pull down the tower of white light that was erected when the east was called.

Now you must open the circle. Begin in the east. Take up the athame and point it toward the eastern quarter. Devoke the circle, walking tuathail around it, imagining the barrier of light disappearing, returning back into the tip of the athame. Now speak the charm:

"Behold: As above, so below! As
the universe, so the soul! As within,
so without! May the circle be open
but never broken! Merry meet,
merry part, and merry meet again!"

Now have everyone cleanse and release all excess energy.

• • • •

Act of Power #2
Seed Planting

For this act of power you will need a packet of seeds and a number of small individual planting cups filled with potting soil. All of this can be obtained from your local garden center.

Flower seeds would be a good choice for this act of power, although the seeds can be any kind of common garden plant. Whatever you choose, you should make sure it is a plant that is easy to take care of, since not everyone is equally good at or inclined to gardening.

Before ritual, open the packet of seeds and fill a small bowl with the contents, then place this on the altar. Fill the planting cups with soil and place them on the altar as well. Make sure you have as many planting cups as you need for the number of people likely to attend. If you are not sure how many people to expect, it is better to have too many planting cups rather than too few.

When you have cast your circle and invoked and spoken a bit about Ostara, take up the bowl of seeds from the altar. Speak about the nature of seeds and their relevance to the holiday. You might say something along these lines:

"At this time of year, we turn our thoughts to new beginnings. The waxing sun heralds the beginning of the growing season, and new life abounds on all sides. The plants are greening, the animals are becoming more active—all that has slept through winter is awakening.

What better symbol of this time of year than the seed? For a seed is all about potential. Planted in the warm and nurturing earth, gently coaxed by the heat of the sun, it has every chance to grow and blossom in the garden of life. But left to lie as it is, without care and guidance, it will remain a seed and never know what could have been.

It is the same with us and our lives. Our hopes and dreams are all about potential, but they must be nurtured and shepherded along if they are ever to move from potential into being. We must set our intent and focus our will, putting our energy behind our goals if we wish to see them blossom. Only then may the seed of hope fulfill its destiny and become the flower of manifestation.

Therefore at this time of year we honor the return of life to the land and seek to imitate it in our lives, blooming in our turn and bearing fruit in our season. Consider the seed—for all things begin as a seed: the seed of life, the seed of thought, verily the seed of action. Let us therefore plant our seeds consciously and with care."

Place the seeds in the center of the circle, set them upon the floor, or have each person put a hand under the bowl and all hold them jointly. Bless the seeds. You might do it like this:

Ostara

"Behold, in the name of the Goddess and of the God, may these seeds be blessed!"

Imagine the light of Deity coming down upon the seeds, filling them.

Now ask each person to take some seeds.

Pass out the planting cups. Explain what is to be done. You might say:

"Now we are going to plant our seeds, so that new life can grow. Make a little hole with your fingers and put your seeds into the earth. Then gently cover them over. As we plant these seeds, let us think

121

about the seeds we wish to plant in our lives, to grow in coming months. What do you wish to do in the next few months? Is there anything you wish to accomplish? Anything you'd like to change? Think of these things as you plant your seeds. Focus upon them, so that the seed is imbued with the thought. As the year moves forward, the seeds will grow, and as they grow they will help carry our goals forward."

Plant your own seed along with everyone else, and think about what you wish to accomplish in the coming months.

Now place the cups in the center of the circle. Have everyone focus energy into them, see them glowing with light and power. Remind everyone to think about what they want to manifest as the plant grows.

You may wish to chant and dance around the seed cups now, to strengthen the energy you are raising. If so, a good chant might be:

"Protected by the earth
Inspired by the sun
Blessed be the seeds that grow
Arise and blossom every one!"

Now finish the act. Focus all of the energy into the seeds and say something to this effect:

"May these seeds be blessed;
may they carry our will forward.
Even as these seeds grow, so
too shall our wishes be made
manifest. Goddess and God we
pray you lend your strength to
ours, as we bless these seeds to
their purpose! So mote it be!"

Explain to people that they will take the seeds home with them after the ritual, and should take care of them as described on the seed package, transplanting them to a pot or the earth when appropriate.

. . . .

Variation #1

One variation on this act of power is to use a packet of mixed flower seeds, so that not everyone gets the same thing. Then you can do divination by the kind of flower each person gets, although this will be evident only much later when the flowers bloom. The kinds of flowers each person has will indicate the success and outcome of their particular manifestation. You can divine the flowers by color or by type as you desire, but as there are likely to be several types together, you will need to consider

their meaning as a whole in order to get a good interpretation from them.

• • • •

Variation #2

A second variation on this act of power is to have a number of packets of different types of seeds. Place them all in a basket and have each person close their eyes and choose a packet at random. Again you would divine the flower by color or type to shed light upon factors affecting the person's manifestation. Unlike variation #1, this allows the flowers to be divined immediately after they are drawn but requires the purchase of numerous packets of seeds.

• • • •

Variation #3

Another variation that you might make in this act of power is to use a visualization before, or instead of, the dancing and chanting to focus the energy. Have everyone place their planting cups in the center of the circle. Then have them visualize. You might lead them like this:

"Imagine your seed; see it there in the dark earth within the planting cup. Imagine the seed glowing and shining with light. See the light shining forth like a sun within your seed. Into that light place strength and love and peace. Think now

of what you wish to manifest for the coming months. Imagine it strongly; imprint it upon the seed.

Now imagine the seed beginning to sprout, sending up a tender shoot. See the shoot growing upward, poking tentatively out of the dark earth. See the shoot growing upward—growing thicker, stronger, becoming a stem and sending forth leaves. Now a bud appears, a delicate bud of green. The bud unfolds, revealing petals, spreading forth as a flower. So, too, may our wishes spread out and bloom as the weeks go forward. Even as these plants grow, so may we also grow and prosper."

Ostara

• • • •

Variation #4

A final variation on this act of power is to keep the plants at the temple rather than to have people take them home. Of course, this only works if you yourself are inclined to gardening. In such a case, one or more special pots might be prepared for the purpose and used in the ritual in place of individual planting cups. Or if you are doing ritual outdoors, you can plant the seeds directly in the earth—perhaps around the perimeter of the circle.

Lady Traci of Holy City Temple did this one year, preparing four special pots: one for each airt. People were instructed to plant their seeds in the pot whose direction best corresponded to the nature of the manifestation. The pots then adorned the temple's outdoor ritual ground throughout the growing season.

This has the benefit of decorating the temple and is also good for bonding, because as the year goes forward people will see their plants growing in the temple precincts each time they come.

• • • •

Act of Power #3
Fire Jumping

Our third act of power for Ostara is very ancient. It is an act of purification by jumping through the flames. In ancient times, people jumped over bonfires at this time of year in order to leave the energies of winter behind in the flames, as well as to symbolically leave behind aspects of their lives they wished to change. Jumping over the bonfire was also thought of as encouraging the plants to grow due to the high leaps of the jumpers, and consequently can also be used for manifestation.

For this act of power you will need a fireproof bowl or cauldron. Place this in the middle of the circle. If you are indoors

be very careful and use common sense in where and how you set it up. Make sure that the hot bottom of the cauldron is not going to directly touch the floor. A heat-resistant tile or board under the cauldron is a good idea.

In its simplest form the fire can be made by placing one or more lighted candles in the cauldron. The number and color of the candles will influence the energy. Four candles in quarter colors will incline to stimulate stability. This is a fairly sedate version of the rite, and is the origin of the old nursery rhyme:

"Jack be nimble, Jack be quick
Jack jump over the candlestick."

Another way of doing the rite is to put one or more lit incense charcoals in the cauldron and place powdered incense on it. This will give you more smoke than fire, but the idea is the same.

These are both good ways to do the rite if you are indoors and cannot have much of a fire. If you are outdoors of course you can have more of a fire—though you must still be careful. Commercially available paraffin campfire buckets are excellent for this purpose as they are small and self-contained, and are very easy to take care of.

In any event, your fire should be small enough to jump over easily, especially if the people present are less than athletic.

To begin, pass out pens and slips of paper to all present. Have everyone think of and write on the paper something they wish to release and leave behind them. When everyone has finished writing, collect the pens and set them aside. Have the people hold on to their paper.

Begin to dance deosil around the circle. Instruct the people to focus on the fire and send it energy. You might want to lead them in a chant. A good chant might be:

> "O, the sun comes up at
> the break of day
>
> And the equinox breaks
> old winter's sway
>
> May the fires carry my ills away!
>
> As I jump through the flames
> with the Young God."

As the group continues dancing, each person should take a turn. One at a time, have each person go to the center of the circle and place their paper into the fire, taking a moment to focus on releasing what is written on it before jumping over the fire. Then they should return to the dance.

When everyone has burned their paper and jumped the fire, lead them in jumping over the fire twice more or as many times as people wish.

When you feel that people have danced enough, stop the dance and stand in a circle around the cauldron. Have everyone focus energy into the cauldron right away. You might lead them like this:

> "Now focus your energy into the
> fire. See the fire glowing brighter,
> brighter than its natural light.
> Imagine it glowing with energy,
> strong and pulsing: stronger
> and stronger. Think about what
> you have released. Know that
> it is gone and will be with you
> no longer! See the fire glowing
> brighter and brighter, the energy
> stronger and stronger, and send it
> forth into manifestation—now!
> And release the energy all at once."

Say a final affirmation to emphasize the full manifestation of the releasing:

> "And it is so. We have made
> our releasing and left that
> which we have released
> behind us in the flames to be
> transformed. So mote it be!"

All: *"So mote it be!"*

Now continue with the rest of your ritual.

Ostara

· · · ·
Variation

Instead of having people write something they wish to release, have them write something they wish to manifest instead. The technique is otherwise the same, but the focus now is on creating rather than releasing.

You might wish to select a different chant, however. Perhaps:

"Jump the fire—leap and go!
Think of what you'd like to grow!
Make a wish and make it so!
Jump the fire—leap and go!"

It should be noted that while fire jumping is particularly associated with Ostara and to some extent with Bealteine, it can be and often is used at other Sabbats as well. It is an excellent ritual technique for either releasing or manifesting.

Chapter
VIII

Bealteine

Bealteine is the great festival of life. It is the polar opposite of Samhain, the great festival of death.

Flowers and foliage are very common decorative elements for Bealteine. These may be found in wreaths, headdresses, garlands, and May baskets, as well as altar decorations. Many colored spring flowers are often used—at other times red and white roses or red roses and white lilies are used to symbolize the union of God and Goddess.

Polar colors such as red and white, green and red, or blue and yellow are a very common theme, emphasizing the divine union. Also, because of the emphasis on divine union, Bealteine is strongly associated with fertility and sensuality. For that reason, symbols that reflect love and merrymaking are often an element. The maypole itself is the ultimate Bealteine fertility symbol, whose symbolism is hard to miss.

Always the emphasis at Bealteine is on color and merriment, because it is the

festival of life. In decorating your ritual space for Bealteine, use items that suggest renewed and abundant life, rejoicing, and celebration.

• • • •

Air

Begin by clearing and releasing all excess energy, as usual. Release all tensions and anxieties. Just let them flow through and out of your body like a gentle wave of energy, exiting through the soles of your feet.

Begin by cleansing the salt; make three tuathail circles above it while visualizing yellow-white light. Imagine the light forcing out all negative or unfocused energy from the salt. Speak words to the effect of:

"Behold, I exorcise you, O creature of earth, casting out from you any impurities that may lie within."

The salt is then blessed; make three deosil circles above it while visualizing blue-white light. Speak words to the effect of:

"And I do bless and charge you to this work!"

Next cleanse the water, making three tuathail circles above it while visualizing yellow-white light forcing out all negative energy. Speak words to the effect of:

"Behold, I exorcise you, O creature of water, casting out from you any impurities that may lie within."

Then bless the water, making three deosil circles above it and visualizing blue-white light. Speak words to the effect of:

"And I do bless and charge you to this work!"

Address the salt, saying:

"Behold, the salt is pure!"

Then address the water, saying:

"Behold, the water is pure!"

Now take three pinches of salt and add it to the water, saying something like this:

"Purity into purity then, and purity be blessed!"

Taking the mixed salt and water walk deosil around the ritual space, aspersing the area while doing so. Visualize yellow-white light filling the area and forcing out all negative or unfocused energy. Say something like:

"I cleanse you . . . I cleanse you . . . I cleanse you . . ."

When finished aspersing, return the salt and water to the altar.

We will now cast the circle. For this ritual we will cast the circle with the athame or with a ritual sword. If you do not have an athame or prefer not to use one, the wand could also be used—or a crystal, or even your finger.

Begin in the east. Take up the athame and point it outward, visualizing a beam of white light shooting from the athame's tip to what will be the outer edge of the magic circle. Now begin to walk deosil around the circle, imagining the beam of light "drawing" a boundary of light around the circle's edge. As you walk, imagine the boundary growing brighter and stronger, becoming a wall of white light. As you come back around to the east, completing the circle, see the boundary become a solid circle of light around the ritual area. Make this as strong as you can. As you are doing this, you may wish to charge the circle by saying something like:

> *"Behold, we do cut apart a place*
> *between the realms of humankind*
> *and of the Mighty Ones: a circle*
> *of art to focus and contain the*
> *powers we shall raise herein! The*
> *circle is cast! So mote it be!"*

All: *"So mote it be!"*

Fire

In this ritual we will invoke the quarters using animal imagery. Using animal guardians at the quarters is a very ancient idea, and is especially good if you have a shamanic bent.

Begin in the east. Use a wand, sacred tool of fire, or if you prefer use your fingers. Raise the wand, imagining as you do so a column of pure white light arising in the east, at the border of the circle. See the column as strong and pure and filled with energy. Say something like:

East

> *"I do invoke you, O golden eagle*
> *of the east! Power of air! The*
> *beating of your wings raises*
> *the winds of inspiration and*
> *enlightenment! Share with us*
> *your powers of conception and*
> *delineation, that we may have*
> *clarity of mind and thought. Join*
> *us, be with us, guide and inspire*
> *us in this our holy ritual! We*
> *bid you hail and welcome!"*

All: *"Hail and welcome!"*

Now move to the next quarter. Again raise the wand and imagine a column of pure white light arising in the quarter. Say something like:

Bealteine

129

South

"I do invoke you, O red dragon of the south! Power of fire! You breathe forth the flames of passion and manifestation! Share with us your powers of creativity and courage that our actions may be confident and effective! Join us, be with us, guide and inspire us in this our holy ritual! We bid you hail and welcome!"

All: *"Hail and welcome!"*

Now move to the next quarter. Again raise the wand and imagine a column of pure white light arising in the quarter. Say something like:

West

"I do invoke you, O blue dolphin of the west! Power of water! From your blowhole you spout waves of sensitivity and compassion! Share with us your powers of love and empathy that our emotions may be open and free-flowing! Join us, be with us, guide and inspire us in this our holy ritual! We bid you hail and welcome!"

All: *"Hail and welcome!"*

Now move to the next quarter. Again raise the wand and imagine a column of pure white light arising in the quarter. Say something like:

North

"I do invoke you, O black bear of the north! Power of earth! You make your home in the cave that resonates with wisdom and understanding! Share with us your powers of focus and integration that we may be steady and well grounded! Join us, be with us, guide us and inspire us in this our holy ritual!"

All: *"Hail and welcome!"*

Now it is time to invoke Deity. Since Grand Sabbats are lunar ceremonies, the Goddess will be invoked first. In this case we shall invoke the Goddess not in any particular personal form but in her archetype as Mother—in this sense, as the youthful Mother of all growing things. You will remember from First Degree studies that some personal forms of this archetype include Isis, Ishtar, and Cybele.

The priestess raises her arms to call upon the Goddess. She might say something like:

Priestess: *"O Mother Goddess! Giver of Life and Author of Existence! From your endless bounty you create and sustain the universe, and us, your children. Holy Mother, at this time of greatest rejoicing, we call to you and do invoke you! Be with us, we pray. Share with us our happiness and accept our love and thanks for all you bring to us. Divine and Bountiful One, we bid you hail and welcome!"*

All: *"Hail and welcome!"*

Now imagine the Goddess entering the circle. Imagine it in any way that makes sense to you—perhaps by imagining the Goddess in human form, or as a shower of glittering light, or as a ball or tower of light appearing in the circle.

Now let us invoke the God in his archetype as Lover. You will remember from First Degree studies that some personal forms of this archetype include Horus, Tammuz, and Attis.

The priest raises his arms to call upon the God. He might say something like:

Priest: *"O God, we do invoke you in your form as Lover. Divine Consort and helpmeet of the Goddess. Lord of Life, God of the sun and spirit of the growing things, we invite you to join us in this most holy rite that honors your union*

with the Mother! From her and for her you were created: her son, her brother, and her consort. Your union brings fertility and life to the world! O God, we bid you hail and welcome!"

All: *"Hail and welcome!"*

Now visualize the God entering the circle. Finally, invoke the ancestors. You might say something like:

"O mighty ancestors, beloved ones who have gone before, we invoke you and ask you to join us and to bless us! Ancestors of the Correllian Tradition, priestesses and priests, mothers and uncles of the lineage, spiritual family that aids and supports us—lend us your inspiration and your love, your guidance and your aid this night, we pray. Beloved ones, we bid you hail and welcome!"

All: *"Hail and welcome!"*

Bealteine

• • • •

Spirit

Begin by discussing the nature of the Bealteine festival. Like all Sabbats, Bealteine has many aspects you can talk about. In discussing the nature of Bealteine, you might say something like:

"We come together this night to celebrate the feast of Bealteine. Now begins the Light half of the year. The light has been returning since Yule, beginning as a spark in the dark of night and growing stronger and brighter through the months. Now the Goddess, Lady of Life, unites with the Lord of the Sun, who has come into his glory. Their loving union will lead us on to the fruitful months of summer. If Samhain is the feast of death and the spirits, Bealteine is the feast of life and the living. It is a time for joy and love. Let us therefore have love in our hearts as we celebrate this most sacred ceremony!"

. . . .

Act of Power
May Queen and May King

Our first act of power for Bealteine involves the May Queen and May King. The May Queen and May King symbolically represent the Goddess and the God during the Bealteine rites.

The May Queen and May King should be selected prior to the beginning of the ritual.

The May Queen and May King may be selected in any of a number of ways. One way is to draw lots, with all the women present drawing lots for May Queen and all the men drawing lots for May King. Another way to select a May Queen and May King is to assemble all of the women and toss a flower wreath or bouquet; whoever catches it becomes the May Queen. Then assemble the men and toss a ceremonial wand in the same way; whoever catches it becomes the May King. Still another way is to choose the first woman to arrive as May Queen and the first man to arrive as May King.

All of these ways to choose the May Queen and May King are at random, and the person selected is considered to have been chosen by Spirit and to receive a special blessing for the year. The downside to all of these selection methods is that there is no time for advance preparation, and the May Queen and May King must be coached with short notice on anything they need to do, and they will probably need note cards for any speaking roles in the ritual.

These drawbacks can be avoided by simply appointing someone to the role ahead of time, although this removes the aspect of special blessing.

Costuming the May Queen and May King can be a lot of fun if you are into that sort of thing. Special robes, tabards, or masks may be used. Floral wreaths are nice for a headdress—red for him, white for her. But of course no special costume is necessary.

Open your ritual as usual. Cast the circle, invoke, speak about the holiday. Then let the May King step forward. He should already have with him an athame or ritual sword, or else take it from the altar at the appropriate moment. Let the May King say something like this:

May King: *"I am the Lord of Life. The sun is my body, no less than the greening trees and fields, or the blue sky with its passing clouds. The sun is my body, and his rays are my passion; his light, my joy and inspiration. In Midwinter I am reborn, and in the season of the ram I arise and unfold in the sprouting seeds and growing plants. I call to my sister the Maiden, 'Come and play with me!' I warm her cold earth with my rays and melt the ice that had held her. I touch her with my light, and awaken her loving heart. She turns to me and her heart is open. Now I come for her, to join with her and stand with her in this season of life."*

Let the May King now hold up the athame as he continues to speak:

May King: *"My blade is the Phallus of Light, the Staff of Secullos, the Great Lightning Bolt that defines the borders of all things, The Horizon of Space and Time, of Night and Day, of Life and Death. Only through Light is one thing distinct from another, for all is as one in the darkness. Light makes us individual and specific. Light is as the blade that separates. Be this blade now blessed in the name of the Lord of Life, and may it be a source of never-ending blessing!"*

The May King now blesses the athame, calling down upon it a column of light from the heavens and filling the athame with strong, vital celestial energy until it is full and shining forth with light in all directions. If the man enacting the role of May King is not experienced enough in energy working to do this, a more experienced priest may help him.

Now the May Queen comes forward and speaks. She should already be carrying the chalice, or else take it from the altar at the appropriate point. The chalice should be full of water, juice, or wine, preferably something red like cranberry juice or a red wine. The May Queen might say something like:

May Queen: *"I am the Lady of Life. The earth is my body, no less than the moon*

Bealteine

133

and stars or the vastness of space. The earth is my body and the plants and animals that live upon her are my children. Through the cold of winter I have lain sleeping, protecting the roots and seeds beneath my blanket of white. The groundhog called my name and I awoke as the Maiden. The ice cracked and the first buds appeared. The singing of birds filled the mornings. Feeling the warmth of the waxing sun I arose. I guided the tender shoots and painted the newborn flowers with the colors of dawn. I hear my brother's voice, and I am filled with love. The field's flower and summer comes!"

Let the May Queen now hold up the chalice, as she continues along these lines:

May Queen: *"My chalice is the womb of creation, the cauldron of plenty that can never be emptied, the white hole that gives rebirth to the matter that the black hole has swallowed. It is the dark cave from which all things come and to which all things in time return. In the Darkness that is our origin, all is one, undifferentiated and in union. I am one, and in me you are one. Hear my voice, for I dwell within your heart. Be this chalice then blessed in the name of the Lady of Life, and may it be a source of union and of love!"*

The May Queen now blesses the chalice, calling up a column of energy from the earth and filling the chalice with strong, peaceful earth energy until it is glowing with light and power. If the woman enacting the role of May Queen is not experienced enough in energy working to do this, a more experienced priestess may help her.

The May Queen and May King now come together. The May Queen holds out the chalice. The May King holds aloft the athame. They speak the charm:

May King: *"The God is not greater than the Goddess."*

May Queen: *"Nor is the Goddess greater than the God."*

May King: *"But both are equal."*

May Queen: *"And neither is complete without the other."*

The May King now plunges the athame into the chalice.

All: *"So mote it be!"*

The chalice is placed upon the altar with the athame still in it. It can be used later for the toast, as it is now blessed.

The May King and May Queen now join hands and dance in a deosil circle three times around. If there is a maypole, they should dance around it; if not, they should simply dance in the center of the circle.

This is a good prelude to the maypole dance. If you do not wish to follow with a maypole dance, you might follow it with dancing and chanting and a simple manifestation, or perhaps a fire jumping similar to that we discussed in the Ostara chapter, or whatever else you wish. It can also stand alone, as shown here.

• • • •

Water

If you used the act of power given above, then the chalice is already blessed and ready to go. If you use a different kind of act of power, then you will need to bless the chalice now. Because Bealteine celebrates the union of Goddess and God, the following might be a particularly interesting way to do it.

This again is our flaming chalice blessing. It is especially apt for Bealteine as it very graphically illustrates, through the image of a flaming liquid, the union of Goddess and God.

Let the chalice be prepared with an alcoholic beverage such as brandy. The priestess or someone else suitable will hold the chalice and represent the Goddess. The priest or someone else suitable will hold a consecrated match or lighter and represent the God.

The priestess will face the people and present the chalice, holding it aloft. She should say something like:

Priestess: *"Behold, the womb of creation! The cauldron of eternity! The circle of life and death that returns ever unto itself!"*

Now let the priest face the people and hold up the consecrated lighting instrument. Let him say something like:

Priest: *"Behold, the phallus of the God! The axis of the planes! The line of time and space that moves ever forward!"*

Now priestess and priest face each other. The priestess continues along these lines:

Bealteine

Priestess: *"In the beginning was the Goddess, and she was alone and without form in the void of chaos. Within her were the seeds of all things that would come later, for hers was infinite potential. And alone with all possibility she dreamed, and wondered about what possibility could become. Dreams moved to plans and plans to action, and behold: from within herself she created the God."*

And the priest might say:

Priest: *"And the God burst forth from the Goddess with a Big Bang, an explosion of fire and light that shot out in all directions! This was the first creation, when God was split from Goddess: Son from Mother, Brother from Sister. And all that was motile, hot, and physical became the God, and all that was stable, cool, and ethereal remained in the Goddess. And the Goddess looked upon the God and she desired him with exceeding desire."*

Let the priestess continue:

Priestess: *"And the Goddess yearned to be one with the God again. But she was told: 'To rise you must fall.' And so she separated the many souls off from herself and sent them into matter—separate from her and yet always connected to her."*

And now the priest:

Priest: *"And thus did Goddess unite with God and thus was the world formed as we know it. For each of us is both Goddess and God, soul and body, joined together in the mystery of life."*

Now let the priest light the match or lighter, and place the flame in the fumes of the brandy so that it is set alight. Be very careful with this.

This will be a very pale flame, delicate and blue, which will endure for a few minutes as it burns away the alcohol in the chalice. Let the priest and priestess continue thus:

Priestess: *"The God is not greater than the Goddess."*

Priest: *"Nor is the Goddess greater than the God."*

Priestess: *"But both are equal."*

Priest: *"And neither is complete without the other."*

Priestess: *"Therefore in the name of the Goddess . . . "*

Priest: *"And in the name of the God . . . "*

Together: *"May this chalice be blessed!"*

Let both priestess and priest now flood the chalice with energy, seeing it filled with the bright, shining light of blessing.

Together: *"So mote it be!"*

All: *"So mote it be!"*

Now make certain that the flame is out. It does not take long to burn itself out, but it may be wise to cover the chalice for a few moments to make sure it is extinguished. Again, be careful with this.

Now pass the chalice deosil around the circle, letting each person drink in their turn. You should go last and offer the final bit to Spirit.

Or if you prefer, you can pass out paper cups and fill them from the chalice, asking everyone to wait and drink at the same time. Make sure to have a cup for Spirit. If you do it this way, you may wish to offer a toast such as:

> "To the Goddess! To
> the God! To us!"

All: *"To the Goddess! To the God! To us!"*

· · · ·
Earth

Now you will close the ceremony and open the circle.

Begin by giving thanks to the ancestors and the deities.

> "Beloved ancestors, you who
> have gone before, your wisdom
> and your example guide us. We
> pray that you will be with us and
> aid us as we go forward, that we
> may call upon the strength and

knowledge of the past, even as we build the future. We thank you for your presence and your aid this night and at all times. May you blessed be in all things. We offer you our love and our respect! We bid you hail and farewell!"

All: *"Hail and farewell!"*

Priestess: *"Holy and bountiful Mother Goddess, Lady of Life and Mistress of Fertility, we thank you for your presence and your aid this night and at all times. We offer you our love and our respect! We bid you hail and farewell!"*

All: *"Hail and farewell!"*

Priest: *"Divine Lover, Consort of Our Lady, Lord of Renewed Life, Master of the Sun and of the Fields, we thank you for your presence and your aid this night and at all times. We offer you our love and our respect! We bid you hail and farewell!"*

All: *"Hail and farewell!"*

Now thank each quarter. Start in the north.

North

"We thank you, black bear of the north! Power of earth! We rejoice in the guidance and the aid you give us! May the blessing be upon you now and always! With love and with respect we bid you hail and farewell!"

All: "Hail and farewell!"

Using the wand, pull down the tower of white light that was erected when the north was called.

Now turn to the west.

West

"We thank you, blue dolphin of the west! Power of water! We rejoice in the guidance and the aid you give us! May the blessing be upon you now and always! With love and with respect we bid you hail and farewell!"

All: "Hail and farewell!"

Using the wand, pull down the tower of white light that was erected when the west was called.

Now turn to the south.

South

"We thank you, red dragon of the south! Power of fire! We rejoice in

the guidance and the aid you give us! May the blessing be upon you now and always! With love and with respect we bid you hail and farewell!"

All: "Hail and farewell!"

Using the wand, pull down the tower of white light that was erected when the south was called.

Now turn to the east.

East

"We thank you, golden eagle of the east! Power of air! We rejoice in the guidance and the aid you give us! May the blessing be upon you now and always! With love and with respect we bid you hail and farewell!"

All: "Hail and farewell!"

Using the wand, pull down the tower of white light that was erected when the east was called.

Now you must open the circle. Begin in the east. Take up the athame and point it toward the eastern quarter. Devoke the circle, walking tuathail around it, imagining the barrier of light disappearing and returning back into the tip of the athame. Now speak the charm:

Chapter VIII

"Behold: As above, so below! As the universe, so the soul! As within, so without! May the circle be open but never broken! Merry meet, merry part, and merry meet again!"

Now have everyone cleanse and release all excess energy.

• • • •

Act of Power #2
The Pole Dance

Our second act of power is the pole dance, or maypole, which may be done following the May Queen and King act of power given above or can stand separately on its own.

The maypole is a very ancient tradition, and is perhaps the most famous of the many traditions surrounding Bealteine. Although clearly Pagan in symbolism and meaning, the maypole was, and in some cases still is, enacted as a spring rite by people of many religions.

The pole for the maypole represents the God in his form of Lord of Vegetation. From the most ancient times a tree has often been used to represent the God, and this is the origin of both the maypole and the Yule tree.

A maypole is relatively easy to make. What you need is a tall pole with a secure base. If you are making an outdoor maypole, the taller the better: it should be at least twelve feet high. If the maypole is

shorter than twelve feet high, the ribbons are likely to come out tangled—of course sometimes this is half the fun, so don't let a need for a shorter maypole discourage you.

An indoor maypole presents a number of problems not encountered with an outdoor pole, but these don't make it impossible. A chief problem is that you need to have it in a room large enough and empty enough to leave space for the dance. Moreover, the height of the pole is limited by the ceiling of the room, but if you have a room big enough and don't mind a shorter pole that may tend to tangle more, there is no reason you can't do an indoor maypole.

Maypoles are best constructed from wood, of course, with a four-by-four from the local lumberyard being ideal. However, other materials can also be used, such as PVC piping or used cardboard carpet rollers that can sometimes be obtained from carpet shops. The base can be made in a number of ways that we will not enumerate here, but it must be large enough to hold the pole steady but not so large as to interfere unduly with the dancing.

A ring must be mounted near the top of the maypole to which the ribbons may be attached. Traditionally, the ribbons are red (for men) and white (for women), and ideally they should be about two or three inches wide. The length depends on the height of the pole and the desired width of the circle of dancers. Measure the ribbon by extending it from the top of the pole to where the dancers will stand at the start of the dance.

Some people prefer to use many colors of ribbon, an allusion to the many colors of spring and summer, but this makes the moves of the dance a bit harder for first-timers to understand, as you will see. One can also use narrow ribbons, but these again are more likely to tangle during the dance.

A chaplet of flowers represents the Goddess. This is placed over the top of the pole, and is raised when the ribbons are outstretched at the start of the dance. As the dance progresses the chaplet will be lowered down the pole as the circle of dancers narrows, representing the divine union. This is very poetic but a bit complicated, so if you choose not to use the chaplet then the circle to which the ribbons are mounted can represent the Goddess.

You should lead into the maypole by explaining its symbolism and relevance. Then you will invariably have to explain the dance to the people. The dance is not hard, but if you have never done it before, it may take some getting used to.

Have everyone take one ribbon and then form a circle around the maypole. The ideal situation is to have an equal number of women and men arranged alternately around the circle. This is not always possible, as sometimes you will not have an equal number of men and women, in which case simply alternate the red and white ribbons around the

circle independent of gender. Sometimes, too, you will not be able to have an equal number of people. In this case you should consider stepping out yourself, so that the number becomes even again, since an unequal number makes the dance much harder.

Have those with red ribbons face deosil and those with white ribbons face tuathail. This is the direction they will dance in. Now when the signal is given, the dancers begin moving in their direction. When the dancers meet, the white dancers raise their ribbons and the red dancers pass under. The dancers continue on; the next time they meet, the red dancers raise their ribbons and the white dancers pass under. The dancers continue around the circle in this way, alternatively raising their ribbon or passing under the others' ribbons. You will want to lead the people through a brief practice run of this once or twice before beginning in earnest, unless everyone present has done it many times.

The last thing to do before the actual dance begins is to place the chaplet of flowers on the pole. The ribbons, held taut by the dancers, will hold up the chaplet until the dance begins.

Now give the signal and let the dance begin. As the dance progresses, with dancers weaving over and under, the ribbons will weave around the pole and the chaplet will slowly descend. It sounds very simple, but it rarely is. Sometimes it comes off well; other times it descends into a happy chaos. People will enjoy it regardless.

You may want to have a chant while the dance is going on. If so, a good chant might be:

"O, honor the Mother
and Father of us all

For summer is a-come unto day

As we dance in a circle
around our tall maypole

On this merry morning of May!

Oh the pole is like our Father
upright and hard as all

For summer is a-come unto day

And the chaplet's like our
Mother in bridal flowers withal

On this merry morning of May!

May Lady and Lord bring
blessings to us all

For summer is a-come unto day

For as the ribbons wrap around
the chaplet comes to fall

On this merry morning of May!"

As the dance progresses, the ribbons will wrap tighter and tighter to the pole, narrowing the circle of the dance until people are right up to the pole. At that point, the ends of the ribbon will be tied off around the pole.

When you have reached this tying off stage, instruct the people to concentrate on something they wish to manifest. You might do it like this:

"Now as you are tying off your
ribbon, think of something you wish
to manifest in your life. Think of it
and make it clear in your mind."

When the last person has tied off their ribbon, have everyone join hands around the pole. You might continue:

"Now let us become aware of our
heart chakra. Imagine a ball of clear
white light in the heart chakra. See
it glowing, shining strongly within
you. And from your heart chakra
now send your energy into the
maypole, and as you do so focus on
that which you wish to manifest. See
the energy entering the pole. See the
pole glowing with energy. Let the
light fill the pole. Let the light shine
out from the pole in all directions.
See it become a column of white light

filling and surrounding the pole, and focus upon what you wish to create:

Holy Mother Goddess, Holy Father God, we ask you to join us, to lend your strength to ours. May your strength support us as we send forth our will to create our wishes in the world. Behold, by our will, with harm toward none. So mote it be!

Now imagine the light moving upward and into manifestation. See it rising up, up. We release it into being so that it may take shape in the material world!"

Imagine the light rising upward, and all raise hands as it does so. Now continue with the rest of your ritual.

It should be noted that a maypole is only a maypole on Bealteine—otherwise it is a ring dance. The ring dance is strongly associated with Bealteine but is also appropriate at either Ostara or Midsummer. Not only is the ring dance appropriate for any of these Sabbats, but some temples enjoy it so much that they may do more than one in a year.

• • • •

Act of Power #3
Axis Blessing

This act of power can be done using the maypole if you have one, or a ceremonial staff or wand if you do not have a maypole. It is a blessing delivered using a vertical axis and can make a good ending to the maypole dance, or can be done on its own.

To do this act of power, have everyone focus on the maypole or, in lieu of a maypole, stand in the center of the circle and hold up your staff or wand and have people focus on that. This will be the basis of your axis. Lead everyone in sending energy into the axis. You might say something like:

"At this time of year we are particularly aware of the loving union of Goddess and God. It is this union of yin and yang, Spirit and matter, essence and motion, which creates and sustains our world. From them and from their union come all things: the food we eat, the air we breathe, the bodies through which we experience this world, and this world itself.

Now, when new life is blooming all around us, it is easy to forget that the world is weary and in need of our love and healing energies. With all we are given, let us not forget to give back also. Goddess and God are in all things, but we honor them often as earth and sky. Let us use their forms as earth and sky to pay back a little to them to show our appreciation and our love for them.

The healing of earth and sky is an ongoing process. No one ritual will ever be enough in itself to accomplish this. But every ritual aimed toward healing helps. We are Witches. We are healers. Let us then not forget to help heal what is so important to us. Let us send healing energy to the earth and to the sky that it may add to their regeneration and renewal, that the next generation may have them still, and better than we had them.

Become aware of your heart chakra. See it as a glowing ball of light within your chest: clear, beautiful white light, shining like a sun within you. And in that ball of light feel the love and strength and power of your heart. Feel the energy within you, and when

you feel it strongly, send forth a beam of light to this axis.

And through that beam of light send love and healing energy into the axis, healing energy for the earth and all her creatures. Healing energy that the earth may use as she sees fit, for she knows better than we where the energy is needed.

See the axis fill with energy, glowing with light all along its length. Imagine the energy growing stronger, brighter, beginning to expand beyond the physical form of the axis. See the light spread out from the axis, expanding around it and moving upward into the sky and downward into the earth. See the axis become a column of light.

A column of light rising up, up into the sky and out among the stars. A column of light going down, down into the earth. Rising higher than we can see— extending deeper than we can see.

Now from your heart send forth green healing light into the column. See the column filling with green light—calm, gentle, green light. And in that green light place love and healing for the earth and for the universe. See the column fill with green light, and in that green light imagine tiny, glittering golden stars. Dozens of tiny golden stars dancing within the green light, and as they dance they multiply, becoming hundreds of golden stars, then thousands. See the green light alive with scintillating golden stars, more and more of them until there is more gold than green.

Now see that green light with its thousands of golden stars shoot upward into the sky—and at the same time see it shoot downward into the earth. Imagine the green and golden light filling the sky above us and the land beneath us. Imagine the healing green light with its golden stars going to every place on Earth and in the sky where it is needed, expanding and multiplying as it does so.

O Mother Earth! Father Sky! We offer you this healing energy! Use it we pray for whatever it is needed for, for you know better than we where and how to direct it. Accept and use it we pray, and may it aid in your healing and regeneration!"

Now offer an appropriate chant such as:

"We are one in the circle
united in love!
With the earth below us
and the sky above!
Together we have one will!
One mind! One heart!
And we focus them all
toward our healing art!
Our magic we send forth
in peace and love!
To the earth below us
and the sky above!

Now let us send out the last of the energy—see it shooting up and down from the axis until it is all gone. Now let the image fade."

Now clear and release all excess energy and continue with the ritual.

Chapter

IX

Midsummer

Midsummer, the summer solstice, is the preeminent solar festival. Midsummer celebrates the God at the height of his powers.

Golds, yellows, and oranges are very appropriate color schemes for Midsummer. So is white. All manner of flowers are appropriate, especially in solar colors—but red roses are also sometimes used.

Solar images are often used at Midsummer: sun disks, solar wheels (the equal-armed cross in a circle, ancient symbol of the sun), lion imagery. Phallic symbols are also sometimes used, some more obvious in the symbolism than others.

In Scandinavian countries the pole dance (maypole) is strongly associated with Midsummer, and enacting a pole dance at Midsummer is both appropriate and a fairly common practice. The pole dance is great fun, and even if you just did it for Bealteine you will find that people will usually enjoy doing it again. Also, in

cooler climates Midsummer can be a better time for a pole dance, if it is being held outside.

As always, you want to choose what has meaning to you and the others present. Adapt ideas in a way that helps you feel special about the holiday, and that helps you to make the magical shift of consciousness.

• • • •

Air

Begin by clearing and releasing all excess energy, as usual. Release all tensions and anxieties. Just let them flow through and out of your body like a gentle wave of energy, exiting through the soles of your feet.

Begin by cleansing the salt. Make three tuathail circles above it while visualizing yellow-white light. Imagine the light forcing out all negative or unfocused energy from the salt. Speak words to the effect of:

"Behold, I exorcise you, O creature of earth, casting out from you any impurities that may lie within."

The salt is then blessed. Make three deosil circles above it, while visualizing blue-white light. Speak words to the effect of:

"And I do bless and charge you to this work!"

Next cleanse the water, making three tuathail circles above it while visualizing yellow-white light forcing out all negative energy. Speak words to the effect of:

"Behold, I exorcise you, O creature of water, casting out from you any impurities that may lie within."

Then bless the water, making three deosil circles above it and visualizing blue-white light. Speak words to the effect of:

"And I do bless and charge you to this work!"

Address the salt, saying:

"Behold, the salt is pure!"

Then address the water, saying:

"Behold, the water is pure!"

Now take three pinches of salt and add it to the water, saying something like this:

"Purity into purity then, and purity be blessed!"

Taking the mixed salt and water, walk deosil around the ritual space, aspersing the area while doing so. Visualize yellow-white light filling the area and forcing

out all negative or unfocused energy. Say something like:

*"I cleanse you . . . I cleanse
you . . . I cleanse you . . . "*

When finished aspersing, return the salt and water to the altar.

We will now cast the circle. For this ritual we will use a spiral casting. Have the people assemble at the east and wait until the ritual space is cleansed. Then lead them in, single file: process deosil in a circle around the edges of the ritual space, marking out the circle of art. As you do this, visualize a trail of white light being created behind you. As you come around to the east again, this trail of white light will form a circle. Process around the circle three times, imagining the white light becoming clearer and brighter as you go. As you do this you might want to chant. A good chant might be:

*"The spiral is a circle that
continues past its start*

*Ever rising, weaving, winding!
With the magic of the heart!*

*We spiral round our temple
make it holy, make it ours!*

*And our dancing forms a circle
as mighty as the stars!*

*The spiral is a circle that
continues past its start*

*Ever rising, weaving, winding!
With the magic of the heart!*

*We are one within our circle
with the God and the Goddess*

*Who move through us in the
circle as our circle we now bless!*

*The spiral is a circle that
continues past its start*

*Ever rising, weaving, winding!
With the magic of the heart!"*

After the third time around, stop and lead the people in a visualization to formalize the circle. You might do it like this:

*"Behold, with our steps we have
cast a circle, created a place
between the world of humankind
and of the Mighty Ones. Imagine
it around us. See it as a wall of
light surrounding us. Bright,
shining white light. Imagine it
clearly, strongly: a circle of art to*

*focus and to contain the powers
we shall raise herein. Around,
around, around, about! All good
stay in and all ill keep out!"*

Now invoke the quarters.

· · · ·

Fire

In this ritual we will invoke the quarters
through the forms of the God. This can
be particularly good for the Lesser (solar)
Sabbats or other rituals that honor the
masculine polarity.

Begin in the east. Use a wand, sacred
tool of fire, or if you prefer, use your fingers. Raise the wand, imagining as you do
so a column of pure white light arising in
the east, at the border of the circle. See the
column as strong and pure and filled with
energy. Say something like:

East

*"I invoke you, O God, in your form
as Golden Lord of the East, hero
and Champion of the Goddess,
Lord of the Dawn and of Spring!
Your breath is in the air and the
greening buds of leaves and flowers.
May your wind bring fresh ideas
and inspiration to our circle!"*

Now move to the next quarter. Again
raise the wand, and imagine a column of

pure white light arising in the quarter. Say
something like:

South

*"I invoke you, O God, in your
form as Red Lord of the South,
Lover and Consort of the Goddess,
Lord of Noonday and of Summer!
Your spirit is in the fire and
the growing crops of the fields.
May your flames bring passion
and vitality to our circle!"*

Now move to the next quarter. Again
raise the wand, and imagine a column of
pure white light arising in the quarter. Say
something like:

West

*"I invoke you, O God, in your
form as Blue Lord of the East,
King and Right Hand of the
Goddess, Lord of Sunset and
of Autumn! Your blood is in
the water, in the harvest that is
reaped and in the falling leaves.
May your waves bring empathy
and compassion to our circle!"*

Now move to the next quarter. Again
raise the wand, and imagine a column of
pure white light arising in the quarter. Say
something like:

North

"I invoke you, O God, in your form as Green Lord of the North, Sorcerer and Guardian for the Goddess of the Gates of Life and Death, Lord of Midnight and of Winter! Your flesh is in the earth, the frosted trees and seeds that wait for rebirth. May your soil bring wisdom and understanding to our circle!"

Now it is time to invoke Deity. Since the Lesser Sabbats are solar ceremonies, the God will be invoked first. In this case we shall invoke the God not in any particular personal form, but in his archetype as Lover. You will remember from First Degree studies that some personal forms of this archetype include Horus, Tammuz, and Attis.

The priest raises his arms to call upon the God. He might say something like:

Priest: *"O Mighty God, we invoke you in your name of Lover! Loving and Beloved Consort of the Goddess, Lord of Life and Growth, your fiery passion and shining heart radiate love throughout the universe. Inspire us with your spirit of service and devotion! Share with us your joy in life and living! Be with us, O God, and guide us we pray in this our sacred ritual! We bid you hail and welcome!"*

All: *"Hail and welcome!"*

Now imagine the God entering the circle. Imagine it in any way that makes sense to you, perhaps by imagining the God in human form, as a shower of glittering light, or as a ball or tower of light appearing in the circle.

Now let us invoke the Goddess in her archetype as Mother, in this sense the youthful Mother of all growing things. You will remember from First Degree studies that some personal forms of this archetype include Isis, Ishtar, and Cybele.

The priestess raises her arms to call upon the Goddess. She might say something like:

Priestess: *"O Holy Goddess, we invoke you in your name as Mother! Creator and sustainer of life, source of all fertility and abundance, you nourish and succor us, your children. From you all things proceed and from your loving heart are provided for! Share with us your all-reaching compassion and providence! Inspire us to embrace love for all life! Be with us, O Goddess, we*

pray, in this our holy rite! We bid you hail and welcome!"

All: *"Hail and welcome!"*

Now visualize the Goddess entering the circle.

Finally, invoke the ancestors. You might say something like:

"O mighty ancestors, beloved ones who have gone before, We invoke you and ask you to join us and to bless us! Ancestors of the Correllian Tradition, priestesses and priests, mothers and uncles of the lineage, spiritual family that aids and supports us. Lend us your inspiration and your love, your guidance and your aid this night, we pray. Beloved ones, we bid you hail and welcome!"

All: *"Hail and welcome!"*

• • • •
Spirit

Now discuss the nature of the Midsummer Sabbat. Midsummer, like all Sabbats, has many aspects, and where you put your emphasis is up to you. In discussing the nature of Midsummer, you might say something like:

"We come together at this time to honor the sun at the height of his reign, the longest day of the year. Now the powers of life are at their strongest; for many months they have grown and now they prosper. But from this time forward the days will grow shorter and the powers of life will begin to wane as the harvest comes and the world slips inexorably toward winter. It is always so in life: that when a thing reaches the moment of its greatest perceived perfection, it then begins to change. The only constant in existence is change. Life is growth and transformation. For we see in the handiwork of Goddess and of God—that is, the world around us—that if perfection can be said to exist, it must reside in motion rather than permanence. Let us therefore reflect upon this and not become bound to a particular moment of imagined perfection, but embrace and enjoy the journey that is life."

Act of Power
Incense Circle

For this ritual our act of power will be an incense circle. For this act of power you will need several types of powdered incense and a censer to burn them in. Of course if there are people who are allergic or sensitive to incense, you would not want to use this particular act of power.

What you use for a censer depends in part on where you are. If you are outside you can use a small barbecue grill and barbecue charcoal, along with substantial quantities of the incense, used liberally, a handful at a time. The effect of this can be exceedingly dramatic and atmospheric. However if you are indoors this will not be desirable at all; instead use a small censer, a brass censer, a metal cauldron, or a heat-resistant burning dish with one or more incense charcoals in it, and much smaller amounts of incense used sparingly—a pinch at a time. Be careful with the censer as you do not wish to have an accidental fire.

You should have at least three types of incense whose qualities pertain to different types of possible manifestations. For example, you might use cinnamon for manifestations that involve issues of prosperity, rosemary for manifestations that involve issues of healing, and anise for manifestations that involve spiritual issues. For outdoor use it can be especially nice to use

incenses such as these that are also common cooking spices, since they are usually available in bulk, allowing liberal usage. Of course any of many other incenses with appropriate energies could be used as well.

Start the charcoal in the censer before the ritual begins so that it is good and hot by the time you are ready to use it. Have everyone form a circle around the censer and explain the process. You might say something like:

> *"At Midsummer the sun is at the height of his power. The sun is the lord of the physical world and of manifestation, which is the creation of a desired effect through magic. For this ritual we are going to work with manifestation through fire and air, the diurnal elements associated with the God. As we go forward, be thinking of something in your life that you wish to create or change —something you wish to manifest.*

> *Perhaps you wish to manifest prosperity into your life? Or perhaps abundance, a better job or job situation, the success of some physical goal. We have cinnamon here for that. For prosperity you will use that incense."*

Midsummer

You might wish to indicate or hold up the cinnamon at this time, so everyone knows exactly what it is.

"Or maybe you wish to manifest something regarding healing? An illness or blockage that needs to be cleared, releasing of things outgrown. For healing we have rosemary. Use that incense if you wish to heal something."

Indicate the rosemary.

"Or maybe you wish to manifest something spiritually? Spiritual growth, psychic development, deeper understanding of something— for these we have anise."

Indicate the anise.

"We will go around the circle several times, so we will each have the chance to manifest several things. Think about that which you wish to manifest, and have those things clear in your mind. When it is your turn, take some of the incense that most closely fits your goal, focus on what you wish to manifest, throw the incense on the coals, and say:

'Mine!' Then we will go on to the next person. Here: I will start us."

Demonstrate by focusing on your goal and tossing the appropriate incense onto the charcoal. As you do so, cry, "Mine!" Of course, you could just as easily use any other positive affirmation here that you might wish.

The person deosil to you will go next, and thence around the circle. Go around the circle as many times as you wish; in practice this will depend a lot on how many people are present. If there are many people in the circle, you may only go around twice or three times, whereas if there are only a couple you may wish to do more. If there are too many people present, once may be enough. You want to give each person a chance to do it but not to go so long that you begin to lose their interest.

A great deal of smoke will be generated, and the several incenses will release their competing scents; the effects of both will be very engaging to the senses. In addition, if you add saltpeter or ground eggshells to your incense it will produce exciting sparks as it burns, but if you try this be careful not to add too much.

When everyone has had a chance to throw some incense on the fire, preferably several times, begin a chant. You might also want to join hands and dance around the barbecue/censer. A good chant for this might be:

"Mine! Mine! Mine! Mine!
By my will and by my hand!
I call you to me where I stand!
Mine! Mine! Mine! Mine!
As I will it you will be
I call you to me—come to me!
Mine! Mine! Mine! Mine!
By all the power of three times three
As I do will, so mote it be!"

When you feel that this has gone on long enough, stop the chant and focus the energy. You might lead the people in this way:

"Now let us focus the energy into
the censer—imagine the energy
rushing into the censer. See
the censer glowing and shining
with light! Imagine it like a sun
in the center of our circle, filled
with energy and power. As you
imagine the censer filled with
light, think again about the things
you have manifested. There is
One Power in the universe, and
we are perfect manifestations
of that Power—and as such let
us in this moment manifest our

will, with harm toward none, and
release it into being —now! See
the light grow brighter but smaller,
brighter and smaller, smaller,
until it is gone, released to bring
our will to pass. So mote it be!"

All: *"So mote it be!"*

Now continue with the ritual.

• • • •

Water

For this ritual we are going to bless the chalice using the imagery of the four quarters.

Fill the chalice with the desired beverage.

Select four people to represent the quarters. Have them come forward and form a circle around the chalice. Hold the chalice between them and have each one put one hand on the chalice. Have them bless the chalice along these lines:

East

"In the name of the east and
the element of air may this
chalice be blessed. May this
chalice and all who share in
it be blessed with insight and
inspiration from the east!"

Midsummer

153

South

"In the name of the south and the element of fire may this chalice be blessed. May this chalice and all who share in it be blessed with courage and passion from the south!"

West

"In the name of the west and the element of water may this chalice be blessed. May this chalice and all who share in it be blessed with empathy and compassion from the west!"

North

"In the name of the north and the element of earth may this chalice be blessed. May this chalice and all who share in it be blessed with wisdom and understanding from the north!"

Now pronounce a final blessing upon the chalice, something to this effect:

"In the name of the Center and of Spirit, which is the origin and culmination of the elements, may this chalice be blessed. Divine Mother Goddess, Divine Father God, join us in blessing this chalice—may it be a token of the bond of love between us, and of the bond of love between the elements, the world of manifestation that they form, and ourselves. May the blessing be!"

Now imagine the chalice filling with light. See it glowing and shining with energy, radiating out in all directions.

Let the quarter callers now return to their positions. Give the chalice first to the person who called the east. Let the east drink, then let the chalice be passed from person to person deosil around the circle, each drinking in their turn.

You should go last, leaving some in the chalice to be offered to Spirit.

Or if you prefer, you can pass out paper cups, filling them from the chalice, asking everyone to wait and drink together, saving one cup for Spirit. In this case you may wish to offer a toast, such as:

"To the Lady! To the Lord! To us!"

All: *"To the Lady! To the Lord! To us!"*

Now give thanks.

· · · ·
Earth

Now you will close the ceremony and open the circle.

Begin by giving thanks to the ancestors and the deities.

> *"Beloved ancestors, you who have gone before, your wisdom and your example guide us. We pray that you will be with us and aid us as we go forward, that we may call upon the strength and knowledge of the past, even as we build the future. We thank you for your presence and your aid this night and at all times. May you blessed be in all things. We offer you our love and our respect! We bid you hail and farewell!"*

All: *"Hail and farewell!"*

Priest: *"Divine Lover! Holy Consort of our Holy Goddess! Lord of ever-lasting love, strength, and vitality, we thank you for your presence and your aid this night and at all times. We offer you our love and our respect! We bid you hail and farewell!"*

All: *"Hail and farewell!"*

Priestess: *"Most Beloved Mother Goddess, holy and ever-abundant Womb of Creation! You who created and who sustains all! We thank you for your presence and your aid this night and at all times. We offer you our love and our respect! We bid you hail and farewell!"*

All: *"Hail and farewell!"*

Now thank each quarter. Start in the north.

North

> *"We thank you, O God, in your form as Green Lord of the North: Sorcerer, Lord of Midnight and of Winter! We are grateful for your guidance and your aid in this our holy ritual! From our hearts—with love and with respect, we bid you hail and farewell!"*

All: *"Hail and farewell!"*

Using the wand, pull down the tower of white light that was erected when the north was called.

Now turn to the west.

West

> *"We thank you, O God, in your form as Blue Lord of the East:*

Midsummer

King, Lord of Sunset and of
Autumn! We are grateful for
your guidance and your aid in
this our holy ritual! From our
hearts—with love and with respect,
we bid you hail and farewell!"

All: *"Hail and farewell!"*

Using the wand, pull down the tower of
white light that was erected when the west
was called.

Now turn to the south.

South

*"We thank you, O God, in your
form as Red Lord of the South:
Lover, Lord of Noonday and of
Summer! We are grateful for
your guidance and your aid in
this our holy ritual! From our
hearts—with love and with respect,
we bid you hail and farewell!"*

All: *"Hail and farewell!"*

Using the wand, pull down the tower of
white light that was erected when the south
was called.

Now turn to the east.

East

*"We thank you, O God, in your
form as Golden Lord of the
East: Hero, Lord of the Dawn
and of Spring! We are grateful
for your guidance and your aid
in this our holy ritual! From our
hearts—with love and with respect,
we bid you hail and farewell!"*

All: *"Hail and farewell!"*

Using the wand, pull down the tower of
white light that was erected when the east
was called.

Now you must open the circle. Begin
in the east. Take up the athame and point
it toward the eastern quarter. Devoke the
circle, walking tuathail around it, imagining the barrier of light disappearing and
returning back into the tip of the athame.
Now speak the charm:

*"Behold: As above, so below! As
the universe, so the soul! As within,
so without! May the circle be open
but never broken! Merry meet,
merry part, and merry meet again!"*

Now have everyone cleanse and release
all excess energy.

Act of Power #2

Oak and Holly Kings

Our second act of power for Midsummer is a mystery play, the Oak and Holly Kings. You should recognize this theme from Yule, where we spoke of it also.

The idea of the Oak and Holly Kings is that the Young God/Oak King rules the summer months while the Old God/Holly King rules the winter. Each of these is at the height of his power at the respective solstice. But even though he will reign for many months afterward, the respective solstice marks the beginning of his decline in power. Thus while the Oak King is at his height at the summer solstice, he will be declining thereafter. This is dramatized as a struggle between the two forms of the God.

For this act of power you will need three people: one to represent the Goddess, one to represent the Oak King, and one to represent the Holly King. If you are creative and into costuming, their appearance can be made quite dramatic, but this need not be so.

When you have spoken a bit about the holiday, explain the nature of mystery plays. You might say something like:

> *"From ancient times Pagans have used mystery plays to dramatize important aspects of*

theology. It is a kind of allegory, presenting complex ideas in simplified, humanized terms. The point of a mystery play is the underlying ideas that it portrays. Behold now the mystery of the Oak and Holly Kings."

Let the person representing the Goddess step forward. She might say something like:

> *"Behold, I am the Goddess, Mother of all things. From the most ancient times I have existed and unto the farthest future I shall be: indeed, I am beyond all considerations of time. I am existence itself. I experience myself through all things—each of you is part of me. From my bountiful womb all things come forth and to me they shall in their time return. I am the earth, the moon, the universe itself. I am the essence of all things.*
>
> *In my time I was the Maiden, and I painted the sky at dawn and the flowers of the fields with the many colors of my palette. I brought life and joy to the world. I danced with the Young God, Lord of Life. The*

Midsummer

touch of the sun warmed the earth, and life flowered everywhere.

I have become the Mother, and with the God at my side I bring forth the bounty of the earth, so that all creatures may thrive. Enjoy, O my children, the warmth and beauty of these months. Make merry and celebrate the beauty around you. But do not forget to set up a store for the future.

For in my time I shall become the Crone. Although he is at the height of his youthful powers now, the God shall one day die and the earth shall fall to winter. It is ever thus: when the rose is at its most fragrant, it has already begun to rot. No sooner is the fruit ripe than it must fall. When the sun has reached its greatest height at noonday then it will begin to sink ultimately into sunset. So, too, this longest day: from this point of greatest power, the reign of the sun shall diminish and the powers of night increase. Days shall grow shorter hereafter, nights longer. Death shall come to the crops; the

leaves of the trees shall fall. The Young Lord will pass away, and the Old Lord shall reign in his place.

For I am the Goddess and I have two consorts: life and death."

Let now the person portraying the Oak King come forward. Let the Oak King and the Goddess join hands.

Oak King: *"I am the Oak King—Young God of Life, hero and Lover of the Goddess. It is I who make the young plants to bud and flower, I who make the crops grow in the fields. I am the Green Man. I make the forests teem with life. I arose with the ram, and melted the snows of winter that Earth might breathe free. I gently warmed her with the sun's rays and nurtured the seeds that sprouted in my name. The Goddess turned to me in love, and all things were green! Our union made the earth bloom and humankind rejoice. I am the Lord of the sun, and this longest day is the time of my greatest ascendancy. In me all things rejoice, and life is made sweet under my rule."*

Holly King: *"Indeed! I challenge you, O Lord of Life!"*

The Goddess steps back and the two kings engage in a mock struggle. The kings can grapple with each other, have a choreographed mock sword fight, or they can use quarter staves—whatever works best for you. At length the Holly King vanquishes the Oak King, who falls to the floor.

Oak King: *"I am wounded! I am struck! In the midst of my greatest power I am cast down!"*

Holly King: *"It is even so. Now the longest day shall pass, and darkness will begin to overtake the sun. Although he shall yet reign a time, he shall diminish; days shall shorten, nights shall lengthen, summer shall ebb into autumn, and in my turn I shall reign in his place. I am the Holly King, Lord of winter and of night. I am Lord of wisdom and of wealth. I am the Kindly One, Giver of Gifts. In the dark of night, torches shall blaze at my feast, gifts be given, songs sung, and visions sought. The world shall turn in upon itself and rest beneath a blanket of snow. Think upon this, look upon the conquered Lord of Life, and know that all things are transitory. All situations, all possessions, all power shall meet change and fade away. What will you retain? Only the emotions and the wisdom that these things give you—therein lies wealth. The love you know, the joy you experience, the lessons you learn, these things you must prize. Turn your thoughts then to those you love, to the experiences you treasure. Appreciate them. When you go forth from this place, look upon these things with new eyes. Make sure they know you value them. Savor your life, do not rush through it. For when, at the end of your life, you meet me, as Lord of the Gate, that savor shall be what you take with you as you leave this world."*

Now lead the people in a gratitude circle. You might do it like this:

"Let us consider the words of the Holly King. What things in our lives are we most appreciative of? What people do we love most? What experiences have formed us, and what activities do we treasure? When we leave this world, what things will we take with us, stored in our heart? Who and what will we carry forward in our soul? These are the things in our life that we should place our emphasis on—not transitory crises or material possessions. The hustle

Midsummer

159

and bustle of life, the pleasure to be had from things, there is nothing wrong with these. They are there for us to enjoy, to bring gaiety and pleasure to our lives. But they are not as important as what we love, and we will forget these momentary pleasures when the time shall come that we must go. Therefore let us now focus on those things that mean most to us and resolve to show them our appreciation for their presence in our lives.

Divine Mother Goddess, Divine Father God, help us always to be mindful of those things that mean most to us in life. Let us not lose sight of their significance, but treasure and nurture them. Help us to be grateful and to show our appreciation and love, that the bond may be always reciprocal. And as we go forth from this place may we be all the more conscious of these things in our life, and of the important role they play. So mote it be!"

All: *"So mote it be!"*

Now continue with your ritual.

Act of Power #3
Citrus healing

Our third act of power is a spell that is used for a working in which everyone present is focused upon the same goal—for example, the healing of a specific person, or peace in a time of troubles. The spell involves a citrus fruit such as an orange or a lemon. This act of power, which would be appropriate for almost any ritual where such working was desired, is especially appropriate to Midsummer because citrus fruit is normally regarded as a solar symbol.

For this act of power you will need an orange or a lemon, preferably one that is fairly large, and a number of pins—ideally with heads of red, white, or blue.

Begin by discussing the goal that is intended. Have everyone focus upon the goal, visualizing it strongly in their mind.

Pass the fruit around the circle. Have each person hold it for a moment, concentrating upon the goal and visualizing the fruit filled with white light.

Now pass the fruit around a second time, but this time let each person stick a white-headed pin into the fruit, while affirming the group goal. For example, each person might say: *"By my will, may Mary be healed."* Or whatever the goal is.

Send the fruit around a third time, and this time let each person stick in a black-headed pin, while affirming: *"May all block- ages be removed!"*

Then send the fruit around a fourth time, this time sticking in the red-headed pins and affirming: *"By all the power of three times three, as I do will so mote it be!"*

Next, begin to toss the fruit back and forth around the circle, while chanting a simple form of the goal, such as *"heal."* Con- tinue tossing the pin-laden fruit, moving faster and faster. When the energy has built for a bit, let the ritual leader take the fruit the next time they catch it and hold it toward the center of the circle, instruct- ing everyone to focus energy into the fruit, while chanting three more times the word *"heal."* As this is done, the ritual leader gradually raises up the fruit. After the last chanting, let everyone imagine the energy rising higher and higher, taking shape in the astral to become manifest in the physi- cal when the circle is opened.

After the ritual, dispose of the fruit by burying it, or keep it in the temple as it slowly and fragrantly dries.

Midsummer

Chapter
X

Lammas

Lammas is the first of the harvest festivals, Mabon is the second, and Samhain is Harvest Home. Because of this you may wish to decorate your ritual space with a harvest theme for Lammas. Sheaves of grain, ears of corn, and squash and gourds are all very appropriate. Vegetables from the garden are very atmospheric on the Lammas altar. Home-baked bread, particularly in rustic shapes, is very good for Lammas. In former times the first loaves of bread baked from the new harvest would be presented and blessed at this ceremony. It is not uncommon for these loaves to be baked in the shape of the God, whose spirit is believed to be in the grain.

Images of the Great Mother are also very appropriate for Lammas, especially the very ancient and primal ones like the Willendorf or the Nile Valley Goddess.

This is the festival that celebrates the God laying down his life for the people.

The sickle used to harvest the grain, symbolically slaying the God, is therefore also sometimes a prominent theme at Lammas.

As always, use what feels right to you and what helps you get into a magical mood.

• • • •

Air

For this ritual we will cleanse the circle by ceremonial sweeping. Make sure the broom that is used for this has been consecrated beforehand as a ritual tool. The type of broom does not matter; it may be of any type from an ordinary household broom to a special ceremonial broom actually made from the broom plant.

When it is time to begin, have the people assemble *outside* the ritual space and wait while you cleanse the circle. After the space is cleansed they will be brought in one at a time.

You or whoever is going to cleanse the area should begin by sweeping tuathail. Sweep the ritual area thoroughly in this manner. Concentrate on sending out all negative energy from the ritual space, and imagine the negative energy rushing out of the area. Imagine the area being filled with cleansing yellow-white light. It might be appropriate to say something like:

"I cleanse this space . . .
I cleanse this space . . .
I cleanse this space . . . "

When the space has been cleansed, turn and begin to sweep deosil. Now focus on blessing the area and preparing it for the ritual. Imagine the ritual area filling with blue-white light. It might be desirable to say something like:

"I bless this space . . .
I bless this space . . .
I bless this space . . . "

Now place the broom at the altar and bring the people in one at a time. Have the people wait at the boundary of the ritual space until their turn comes. Anoint each person with consecrated oil, using the oil to make the sign of the pentagram or the crescent moon on their forehead or on their wrist. Check beforehand to make sure no one is allergic to scented oil. If anyone is allergic, use something else like olive oil or consecrated water instead. Say something like:

"May you be blessed in the
name of the Old Gods. In
perfect love and perfect trust
be welcomed to this circle."

Then let the person enter and repeat the process with the next, until all have entered.

We will now cast our circle. For this ritual we will cast the circle from hand to hand. To do this, begin by turning to the person deosil to you. Take their hand and say something like:

> "From hand to hand I
> cast this circle."

Or you might say:

> "From heart to heart I
> cast this circle."

Or you might say:

> "In perfect love and perfect
> trust I cast this circle."

Or however you prefer to do it.

Then this person will take the hand of the next person and repeat the same words. The next person will do the same thing, and so on around the circle until it returns to you and everyone is holding hands. Now say something like:

> "Behold, we join together to cast
> this circle, that it may be a token
> of the bond of love between us.
> Imagine the energy running from
> hand to hand, person to person.
> See the energy as beautiful, clear
> white light filled with strength and
> love and power. See the energy

> grow and strengthen. See it begin
> to expand around us, the circle of
> energy moving out around us to
> fill our ritual space and make a
> barrier at its edges. See that barrier
> become a wall of clear, strong
> white light: a wall to contain and
> strengthen our energy as we work.

> Behold, we do cut apart a place
> between the realms of humankind
> and of the Mighty Ones—a circle
> of art to focus and contain the
> powers we shall raise herein! The
> circle is cast! So mote it be!"

All: *"So mote it be!"*

Now release hands and continue.

. . . .

Fire

In this ritual we will invoke the quarters through the forms of the Goddess. This can be particularly good for Grand (lunar) Sabbats, moons, and other rituals that honor the feminine polarity.

Begin in the east. Use a wand, sacred tool of fire, or if you prefer, use your fingers. Raise the wand, imagining as you do so a column of pure white light arising in the east, at the border of the circle. See the column as

strong and pure and filled with energy. Say something like:

East

"We call upon you, O Red Lady of the East! You who took the first action and in so doing set the world in motion. Lady of the Dawn and of all beginnings! Behold, we do invoke you, O Lady of the East, and with you the sylphs and spirits of the air! Come to us! Join us! Lend us your aid and your inspiration in this our undertaking!"

Now move to the next quarter. Again raise the wand and imagine a column of pure white light arising in the quarter. Say something like:

South

"We call upon you, O White Lady of the South! You who united with the God and ensouled the world! Lady of Noonday, Mistress of Fertility and of Fecundity! Behold, we do invoke you, O Lady of the South, and with you the salamanders and spirits of the fire! Come to us! Join with us! Lend us your aid and your inspiration in this our undertaking!"

Now move to the next quarter. Again raise the wand and imagine a column of pure white light arising in the quarter. Say something like:

West

"We call upon you, O Gray Lady of the West! You who govern the cycles of time and rebirth. Lady of Sunset, who gathers home the fruits of creation! Behold, we do invoke you, O Lady of the West, and with you the undines and spirits of the waters! Come to us! Join us! Lend us your aid and your inspiration in this our undertaking!"

Now move to the next quarter. Again raise the wand and imagine a column of pure white light arising in the quarter. Say something like:

North

"We call upon you, O Black Lady of the North! You who were before the first creation and who shall endure beyond all reckoning. Lady of Midnight, you who are the darkness before the dawn. Behold, we do invoke you, O Lady of the North, and with you the gnomes and spirits of the earth! Come to us!

Join us! Lend us your aid and your inspiration in this our undertaking!"

Let the four quarters now be portrayed by four people. Since we are invoking the quarters as forms of the Goddess, it is likely that these will be four women; however, this need not be viewed as a requirement. A man may embody the divine feminine just as a woman may embody the divine masculine, since both polarities are present in all things. The four people may be costumed for the parts or not as desired. Most commonly you would have had these same four people invoke the quarters as well as personifying them in the dance that follows, but this, too, need not be a requirement. If you do not have four people to do this, then you should omit the physical dance and use only the spoken parts with one or two people taking all the parts.

Have the four quarters now come to the center of the circle and join hands. Let them dance deosil in the center of the circle singing an appropriate chant, such as:

"Air! Fire! Water! Earth!
Air! Fire! Water! Earth!
Air! Fire! Water! Earth!
We are one!
We are one!
We are one!"

Now speak the charm:

"Behold: Four queens dance,
and by their dance the world is
formed! As it was in the beginning
the dance of the elements sets
the ritual in motion! Thought!
Action! Reaction! Integration!
An endless cycle of being!

Behold the dance and imagine the
energy raised by its steps! See the
energy arising between the dancers,
shining white and radiating in
all directions. See that light grow
and expand. See it moving out
beyond the dancers, expanding
to encompass them, surround
them, then expanding still farther!
See the light fill our ritual space,
growing brighter and brighter,
expanding farther and farther until
it surrounds the entire ritual space.
See the light form a barrier all the
way around us, a barrier of light. A
circle of art to focus and to contain
the powers we shall raise herein!

Behold! By our will so mote it be!"

All: *"So mote it be!"*

Now it is time to invoke Deity. Since Grand Sabbats are lunar ceremonies, the

Goddess will be invoked first. In this case we shall invoke the Goddess not in any particular personal form, but in her archetype as Mother—in this sense the ruling Mother of the Harvests. You will remember from First Degree studies that some personal forms of this archetype include Isis, Yemaya, and Mati Suira-Zemlya.

The priestess raises her arms to call upon the Goddess. She might say something like:

Priestess: *"Behold! We do invoke you, O beneficent Mother Goddess! Provident Lady of the earth whose bounty sustains her children! Holy Mother, who creates and nourishes all things, from whom all sustenance comes. We do invoke and invite you to join us at this time of thankful celebration! With love and with respect we call unto you and beseech you for your aid and guidance in our holy rite! We bid you hail and welcome!"*

All: *"Hail and welcome!"*

Now imagine the Goddess entering the circle. Imagine it in any way that makes sense to you, perhaps by imagining the Goddess in human form, as a shower of glittering light, or as a ball or tower of light appearing in the circle.

Now let us invoke the God in his archetype as King. You will remember from First Degree studies that some personal forms of this archetype include Ra, Jupiter, and Nodens.

The priest raises his arms to call upon the God. He might say something like:

Priest: *"O God, we do invoke you in your form as King! You who as Consort of the Goddess now lay down your life for her children! With deepest thanks and love we invoke you! You, who turn the Wheel and in turn are turned upon it! Be with us we pray, O God, and share with us your wisdom and selfless sacrifice as we honor you for your gift! O God, with love and with respect we bid you hail and welcome!"*

All: *"Hail and welcome!"*

Now visualize the God entering the circle.

Finally, invoke the ancestors. You might say something like:

"O mighty ancestors, beloved ones who have gone before, we invoke you and ask you to join us and to bless us! Ancestors of the Correllian Tradition, priestesses and priests, mothers and uncles

of the lineage, spiritual family that aids and supports us, lend us your inspiration and your love, your guidance and your aid this night, we pray. Beloved ones, we bid you hail and welcome!"

All: *"Hail and welcome!"*

• • • •

Spirit

Now discuss the nature of the Lammas Sabbat. Like all Sabbats, Lammas has many aspects, any of which you might choose to emphasize. In discussing the nature of Lammas you might say something like:

"Lammas is the festival of the harvest. At this time the life of the God begins to wane, the days are growing shorter, the crops in the fields are being felled; slowly but inexorably the earth is moving on toward inevitable winter. We think of this as the God laying down his life that all may live. This concept has special significance at harvest time because we are conscious of the sacrifice of the grain and other plants we have raised for food, but in truth it is a constant, for life is

sustained only by death. All living things depend upon death—for all we eat was once alive. Even the plants that thrive on light cannot exist except through the death of others, for the soil in which they grow is composed of decay from generations of dead foliage and the bodies of dead animals. This is a sobering thought and should inspire us not to horror of death but to deepest gratitude. For all things that die, however unwitting at the physical level, have made a choice from their soul. When we speak of the death of the God it is in part to this law of being that we refer. Let us reflect therefore upon all those that have given their lives to our sustenance, as we one day shall in our turn likewise do."

• • • •

Act of Power
Offering First Fruits

Lammas is the ceremony that marks the beginning of the harvest season, and as such it is appropriate to make an offering of the first fruits of the season at this time. This is essentially an offering of thanks for the abundance of the earth and a prayer for a fruitful harvest. It also honors the

death of the crops, which are understood to be living things, and gives thanks for the sacrifice they have made so that we might live.

Select some nice fruits and/or vegetables for the offering and arrange them attractively. Grains such as wheat or corn (maize) are also appropriate. Ideally it is best to use produce that has been grown in a personal, hands-on manner, as in a household garden or a small farm. But not everyone gardens or knows a good farmer's market, and you shouldn't let that stop you. It's the thought behind the offering that counts and the thought is gratitude.

All the food we eat ultimately comes from the earth, some foods more directly than others. As Pagans we should remain mindful of this, and we should not be seduced by the availability of pre-packaged foods into forgetting that all food owes its origin to the earth and represents a gift of life. Yet thanking the earth is only part of the purpose of the offering, for we must also thank the plants themselves and indeed all of the food we eat.

Everything we eat, whether animal or vegetable, was once a living thing. Plants are no less living things than animals; they only experience their life differently. They have all sacrificed their lives for us, and we should honor that sacrifice. It might be argued that the sacrifice is not always willing, and at a conscious level that may be so, but from the level of the Higher Self the sacrifice must be a willing one or it would not have been made. This too is part of what we honor at Lammas.

Therefore prepare your offering with this is mind.

After you have cast the circle, invoked, and spoken about the nature of Lammas, present the First Fruits offering. The presentation can be as creative as you like. You may have a special person designated to present the First Fruits, perhaps costumed for the part with a seasonal tabard or with a wreath of wheat or harvest fruits on their head. Or if your ritual space is large enough, it might be nice to have a bit of a procession, with one or more people ceremonially conveying the First Fruits to the altar, perhaps accompanied by drumming or a harvest chant.

When the offering has been installed at the altar, you might say something like this:

"This is the time of thanksgiving for the harvest to come, when we shall reap the bounty of the earth. In this age of year-round, prepackaged food, we often forget the importance of the harvest and how much we depend upon the earth for life. At this time of year, let us remember that we are all sustained by the

earth our Mother, the physical embodiment of the Great Mother Goddess whose Spirit inhabits all of the galaxies and universes of existence. Let us be thankful for our life, thankful for our food, and thankful for all of the other harvests of our life, through which our existence is enriched. Let us each consider the things that make our lives sweet and give thanks to the Goddess our Mother for them. I myself am thankful for . . . "

Name something that you are thankful for, something that is important to you and that you are grateful to Deity for.

Now go deosil around the circle and have each person name one thing that they are thankful for in life. Depending on the number of people present, you may want to go around the circle more than once but do not make it too long, lest you lose the people's excitement.

When you have all named something you are thankful for, it is time to bless the First Fruits offering. Turn to the offering and speak over it. You might say something like:

"Holy Mother, on this most sacred day of Lammas we honor you as the source and sustenance of all life.

Lady of the Sickle, who provides for her children that they may not starve in the months ahead, we thank you with all our hearts.

It is you who ordain the cycle of life and death upon which existence depends and to which all things are bound, even the God, your Consort, who turns the Wheel of Life yet is bound to it also. As the crops fall in the fields, and the sun wanes in the sky, as the foliage begins to turn color in the descent toward winter, the God sinks slowly toward his own death, making his willing sacrifice that all may live. It is even so with all things.

Creator and Destroyer, you have ordained that life must feed on life to live, that the old must die and be transformed so that the new may take shape. We give thanks, O Mother, for the food provided to us through your love and foresight. We thank you, and we thank the souls of the food likewise for their sacrifice.

Lammas

171

We are all united in the dance of life and death, and each of us in turn must make our own sacrifice. As these have sacrificed to sustain us, one day we too must make our sacrifice and repay the debt. One day we shall die and our bodies be eaten by worms and creatures of the earth, ultimately becoming part of the soil from which new plants shall grow and upon which new animals shall feed. This is the balance of life. All debts must be repaid. All wheels in their time must turn full circle. When the day comes for us, may we be as gracious in making our sacrifice for them as they have been in making their sacrifice for us.

Holy Mother, bless then this offering in token of this eternal compact! Let it be a bond of love between yourself and us, between ourselves each and the other, and between ourselves and our food that we may ever be mindful of the price of life. In the name of the Lady of Life and Death, may the blessing be upon this offering!"

Now draw down energy into the offering. Imagine it as a shower of light descending upon the offering and filling it totally.

Next, you might want to offer a chant in honor of the Goddess, perhaps accompanying it with a dance. A good chant might be:

"Arise! Arise! And spread your wings!

Mother of all living things!

Arise! Arise! And spread your wings!

Goddess of Eternity!"

When you have finished, direct the energy raised by the chant and dance to the Goddess. You might do it like this:

"Imagine a ball of light building in the center of our circle. See it growing brighter and brighter. Into this ball of light send love and thanks to the Goddess. O Goddess, we ask that you accept this humble offering from us, in token of the love we bear you! May the blessing be upon you now and always!"

Chapter
X

Imagine the ball of light rising up and up and up, until it disappears in a flash of light and goes off to the Goddess. Or alternatively you might imagine the ball of light begin to grow smaller and smaller, until at last it disappears and goes to the Goddess. Either is equally good.

"So mote it be!"

All: *"So mote it be!"*

Now continue with the rest of your ritual.

• • • •
Water

For this ritual we are going to use a group blessing for the chalice. For obvious reasons, this blessing is best with a small group.

Fill the chalice with the desired beverage. Then raise it up and hold it in the center of the circle. Ask everyone present to place one hand upon the chalice and join you in blessing it. You might lead them in the blessing like this:

"Become aware of your heart chakra. Imagine it filled with clear white light, shining and glowing with love and strength. In that light feel the love of Spirit, moving within you.

Now send energy from your heart chakra through your hand and into the chalice—energy filled with love, with joy, with creativity. Fill the chalice with energy. See the chalice filled with shining light, radiating out in all directions, growing stronger and stronger.

O Mother Goddess! O Father God! Beloved ones! Join us we pray in blessing this holy chalice! Lend your energy to ours! Bless this chalice with love and strength! May it be as a bond between us, a bond of enduring love. A bond between yourselves and all of us. A bond between ourselves and one another. Behold! May the blessing be!"

Now fill the chalice with energy. Imagine the chalice filling with more and more energy until it shines with light as though there were a small sun within it.

Now pass the chalice deosil around the circle, letting each person drink. You should go last and offer the final bit to Spirit.

Or if you prefer, you can pass out paper cups and fill them from the chalice, asking everyone to wait and drink together. Make sure to fill one cup for Spirit. If you do this

173

you may wish to offer an appropriate toast such as:

"To the Lady! To the Lord! To us!"

All: "To the Lady! To the Lord! To us!"

· · · ·
Earth

Now you will close the ceremony and open the circle.

Begin by giving thanks to the ancestors and the deities.

"Beloved ancestors, you who
have gone before, your wisdom
and your example guide us. We
pray that you will be with us and
aid us as we go forward, that we
may call upon the strength and
knowledge of the past, even as we
build the future. We thank you
for your presence and your aid
this night and at all times. May
you blessed be in all things. We
offer you our love and our respect!
We bid you hail and farewell!"

All: "Hail and farewell!"

Priestess: "O mighty Mother, we thank
you for your presence and your aid this
night and at all times. You who created

and provide for us. All-bountiful and Open-handed One! We offer you our love and our respect! We bid you hail and farewell!"

All: "Hail and farewell!"

Priest: "O God, King and Consort of the Goddess, you lay down your life in the fields that we might eat! Your light wanes in the sky! But we rejoice and give thanks for your sacrifice! We thank you for your presence and your aid this night and at all times. We offer you our love and our respect! We bid you hail and farewell!"

All: "Hail and farewell!"

Now thank each quarter. Start in the north.

North

"Black Lady of the North! We
thank you for your presence and
your aid in this holy ritual. You
and the gnomes and spirits of
the earth! May there be peace
between us now and always! We
bid you hail and farewell!"

All: "Hail and farewell!"

Using the wand, pull down the tower of white light that was erected when the north was called.

Now turn to the west.

West

"Gray Lady of the West! We thank you for your presence and your aid in this holy ritual. You and the undines and spirits of the waters! May there be peace between us now and always! We bid you hail and farewell!"

All: *"Hail and farewell!"*

Using the wand, pull down the tower of white light that was erected when the west was called.

Now turn to the south.

South

"White Lady of the South! We thank you for your presence and your aid in this holy ritual. You and the salamanders and spirits of the fire! May there be peace between us now and always! We bid you hail and farewell!"

All: *"Hail and farewell!"*

Using the wand, pull down the tower of white light that was erected when the south was called.

Now turn to the east.

East

"Red Lady of the East! We thank you for your presence and your aid in this holy ritual. You and the sylphs and spirits of the air! May there be peace between us now and always! We bid you hail and farewell!"

All: *"Hail and farewell!"*

Using the wand, pull down the tower of white light that was erected when the east was called.

Now you must open the circle. Begin in the east. Take up the athame and point it toward the eastern quarter. Devoke the circle, walking tuathail around it, imagining the barrier of light disappearing and returning back into the tip of the athame. Now speak the charm:

"Behold: As above, so below! As the universe, so the soul! As within, so without! May the circle be open but never broken! Merry meet, merry part, and merry meet again!"

Lammas

175

Now have everyone cleanse and release all excess energy.

- - - -

Act of Power #2
John Barleycorn

John Barleycorn is a name given to the God in his form as Lord of the Crops, just as Green Jack or Green George is a name given to the God as Lord of Foliage.

John Barleycorn is also a name given to images made of grain to represent the God as Lord of the Crops.

There are a variety of ways to make a John Barleycorn image, but for the purposes of this act of power we recommend making him from corn bread, biscuit dough, or sheet cake that is cut, arranged, and decorated in the shape of a man. A large, man-shaped cookie will also work well.

If you are creative, you can have a lot of fun in making your John Barleycorn. You can make him virile and bearded, crowned with a solar crown like Apollo. Or you could make him folksy and cute like a gingerbread man. You could also make him look like the Cerne Abbas giant or whatever else inspires you. But he doesn't need to be complicated or highly artistic, as long as he is recognizably supposed to be the God.

After you have cast the circle, invoked, and spoken about the nature of Lammas, present your John Barleycorn to the people. Again, as with the First Fruits, the presentation can be very creative. Perhaps John Barleycorn can be ceremonially marched around the circle—while a chant is sung extolling the virtues of the God—before he is placed on the altar. A good chant might be:

"There is a spirit in the corn
There is a spirit in the wheat
There is a spirit in the fields
And in everything we eat
It is the spirit of the sun
It is the spirit of the flame
It is the spirit of the God
Of Ten Thousand Names
We honor now the God
In his name as Sacred King
As he lays down his life
With the fields reaping!"

Once John Barleycorn is on the altar, you might say something like this:

"Behold John Barleycorn, spirit of the fields. This is the God, our Lord, who lives in the plants and growing things. He is represented here before us to remind us that we are not the only ones alive. All things that exist live. The plants and animals are no less alive than we. They, too, are manifestations of divinity. They, too, live and

have souls, however different they may be from us. In a world where we no longer see the plants of the field as they grow, where food is more often obtained from supermarkets than from farms, it is easy to forget that life comes with a price. That price is death. All life feeds on life—the plant feeds on the earth, the animal feeds on the plant, one living thing takes sustenance from another living thing, because all things are living. Each thing in its turn makes its sacrifice that the others might live.

At this time of year the God makes his yearly sacrifice. The fields are felled. The autumn overtakes the summer, and the plants begin to die off. The sun slowly sinks toward its death in winter. Let us be thankful then for this sacrifice. Let us not take it for granted, but rejoice in it and be grateful. Let us give thanks for the sacrifice that gives us our food and also for the other harvests of our life, those things that make our lives sweet and through which our existence is enriched. Let us each consider and

reflect upon what we have to be grateful for, and give thanks for it."

As with the First Fruits, you might want to do a gratitude circle at this point. Name something that you are thankful for, something that is important to you and that you are grateful to Deity for. Then go deosil around the circle, each person naming something they are thankful for. Take an appropriate amount of time but remember not to let it get too long, so that everyone stays excited. Boredom is death to a ritual.

When you have completed your gratitude circle, it is time to bless John Barleycorn. Place your hands over the image and speak. You might say something like:

"Oh God, you make your sacrifice for us, that we might live. Let us be ever mindful of it. All things we eat have at one time been living, have made their sacrifice for us. May we in our turn make our sacrifice as graciously. In the name of the Goddess and of the God may this image be blessed as a token of the bond of love and life that exists between all things! So mote it be!"

Now draw down energy into the image. Imagine it as a shower of light falling upon and filling the image. Let the image fill with energy and radiate with light, shining

out in all directions. Next you might want to offer a chant in honor of the God.

Let a woman of the group represent the Goddess in her role as Lady of the Harvest, Creator and Destroyer. Let her use an athame, or if you have one, a ritual sickle. Let her stand over John Barleycorn and say something to this effect:

"I am the Goddess, your Mother. I am the Lady of Life, from me all things are born. I am likewise the Lady of Death; by my will all things die. I brought you into the World, O God, and I take you out of it. For it is my will that for one thing to live another thing must die, that life may continue and never grow stagnant. Therefore, John Barleycorn, I take your life for the sake of my children!"

Using the athame or ritual sickle, the woman portraying the Goddess now cuts up the figure of John Barleycorn. She should make as many pieces as there are people present, plus one more. Then she continues:

"Behold! The God is dead! Long live the God! For death is an illusion; only the body dies, for the soul goes ever onward. Therefore

let all things that live make their sacrifice cheerfully in the knowledge that life never ends. And in token of the bond that is neverending, hear now the sacred words of the charge."

The woman portraying the Goddess now either continues and gives the charge, or another may do it in her place. While this is being read, the body of John Barleycorn should be passed out among the people.

"Hear now the words of the Great Mother, who was of old called many names by the hearts of humankind.

Selv, Diana, Brighid, Laksmi, Yemaya, Kuan Yin, and many others both known and unknown;

Whenever you have need of anything, once in a month and better it be when the moon is full: Then you shall assemble in some sacred place and adore me, the spirit of the moon.

And you shall sing and dance, make music and make love, all in my name. I am the Queen of all the wise. And you shall be free from slavery and as a sign that you are truly free, you shall be open in your rites.

For mine is the ecstasy of spirit, and mine too the joys of the senses, and my law is love unto all beings. Nor do I demand aught of sacrifice, for I am the Mother of All Living and my love is poured out upon creation.

Keep pure this highest ideal, strive ever toward it. Let nothing turn you aside. For mine is the cup of the wine of life, the sacred cauldron that is the grail of immortality.

On Earth I give knowledge of the Spirit Eternal, and beyond death I give peace and freedom—and reunion with those who have gone before.
For I am the Gracious Goddess, who gives joy unto the human heart.

Hear now the words of the Star Goddess in the dust of whose feet are the Hosts of heaven and whose body encircles the universe;

I am the beauty of the green earth and the white moon among the stars, and the Mystery of the waters. I call unto your soul: 'Arise and come unto me,' for I am the Soul of Nature, who gives life to the universe.

From me all things proceed, and unto me all must return. Before my face, O beloved of Gods and humankind, let your Highest Self rejoice, and be enfolded in the rapture of the infinite.

For my worship is in the heart that rejoices, and behold, all acts of love and pleasure are my rituals. Therefore let there be beauty and strength, power and compassion, honor and humility, mirth and reverence within you.

And you who seek to find me in the depths of the sea or the shining stars, know that your seeking will avail you naught unless you know the Mystery;

For if that which you seek you find not within yourself, you will never find it. For behold,

Lammas

I have been with you since the
beginning, and I am that which
is attained at the end of desire.”

Now move on to the toast, using the body of John Barleycorn as the food.

• • • •

Act of Power #3

Earth-healing Stones

For our third act of power for Lammas, we are going to focus on earth healing. Of course earth healing is appropriate at all times, but because Lammas celebrates the harvest and the fecundity of the Goddess in her form as Earth Mother, earth healing is especially appropriate to this holiday.

For this act of power you will need a bowl. In the bowl should be one stone for everyone in the circle.

Begin by passing the bowl around the circle. Ask each person to take out one stone.

When everyone has their stone, you will want to explain how the process will work. You might say something like:

“Hold your stone in your hands
and focus on it. Now think about
the earth. In a way, every stone is
a microcosm of the earth, a little
bit of the earth—often similar in
shape, indissolubly connected to

the whole. Think about the earth
and the difficulties she faces today.
The earth needs much healing,
and there are many different
aspects in which the healing is
needed. Let us each think about
any one aspect of the earth that
is need of healing. It may be an
animal species that is endangered
or it might be environmental
pollution, the destruction of the
rain forests, or even issues of
political freedom. Think about this
and focus on it, any aspect of the
earth that you feel is particularly
in need of healing energy.

Focus intently upon that which
you have chosen for healing.
Picture it clearly in your mind.
Now imagine it being healed—
imagine the healing already
complete and successful.

As you hold your stone, imagine
a ball of white light around it:
clear, strong, beautiful white light.
See the light as bright and full of
energy. And within that ball of
light, think about the thing you
have chosen to heal. See that thing

being healed, becoming whole and healthy and well. Visualize the healing being accomplished."

Now have everyone place their stone at the center of the circle.

Join together in a healing chant. You might also wish to dance, depending upon room and inclination.

A good chant might be:

*"We the children of the earth and sky
Must heal our Mother by and by
With hearts and minds we all must try
To bring her healing—by and by!"*

When you feel that people have danced enough, stop the dance and stand in a circle around the bowl of stones. Have everyone focus energy into it at once. You might instruct them in this manner:

"Let us focus our energy into the stones. See them filled with beautiful, clear white light. Imagine the stones shining with light, radiating in all directions, glowing brighter and brighter. Imagine the stones filled with energy, strong and pulsing, stronger and stronger. Think about what you have healed—concentrate on it and see it whole and healthy!

See the fire glowing brighter and brighter, the energy stronger and stronger, and send it forth into manifestation—now!"

Release the energy all at once.

Now follow with a final benediction, perhaps something like this:

"Divine Mother Goddess, Divine Father God, lend your aid we pray, that these stones now blessed shall carry our working forward into manifestation as surely as the moon passes through her phases, as surely as the planets revolve around the sun, as surely as the rivers run, even so inevitable is the working of our charm! So mote it be!"

The stones have now been blessed.

When the ritual is ended, form a procession and take the stones to the place where you will release them to the elements. Doing so symbolizes the goals becoming manifest. There are several things you can do. You can bury them in the ground or indoors in a pot of soil. You can release them into a river or lake. You can toss them from a hill. It doesn't really matter how you release them, as long as it symbolizes the release of the goals into manifestation.

Lammas

Although I am including this act of power for Lammas, it is of course suitable to any occasion. It can be used for earth healing, which is always needed, or if you prefer you can use it to manifest personal goals instead.

. . . .

Variation #1

A variation on the theme is to have each person take their stone and use it as a talisman, rather than releasing them to the elements. In this way, whether they are used for earth healing, as above, or for more personal goals, by using the stone as a talisman the person will keep the energy around them and be able to add additional energy at will. Moreover, keeping the stone as a talisman will help the person be more mindful of what they have manifested.

. . . .

Variation #2

As we have mentioned, although we give this act of power as an example for Lammas, it is appropriate to any occasion.

Though we have used stones here, many other items can serve just as well. For example, if you are near water, seashells can be very atmospheric. Likewise, if you are in a wooded area, or perhaps if it is winter, pinecones can be very appropriate. In fact, any similar thing will do. Nor must the to-kens used necessarily be natural; charms or medallions can also be used.

If you are using something like pinecones, they can be released by being tossed into a fire. Burning pinecones make a lovely scent. If this act of power is done in a winter ceremony, pinecones can be particularly appropriate and atmospheric.

Chapter
X

Chapter
XI

Mabon

Mabon is the autumnal equinox. It is the time of the waning sun. Days grow shorter, nights grow longer. The fields are being felled as the harvest continues, the life of the God ebbing away. It is the sunset of the year.

Darker colors tend to be used at Mabon: dusk colors, grays, purples, blues.

Because it is an equinox, Mabon is associated with ideas of balance: a particolor theme in polar colors is very appropriate. Purple and green are very fitting. Recall the association of the holiday with Dionysus due to the grape harvest.

Sometimes the harvest theme is stressed, and autumn produce is used to decorate for Mabon: pumpkins, gourds, corn. Haystacks and scarecrows are also sometimes used. Again, another common theme is grapes and grape vines.

Mabon is the last festival of the Wiccan liturgical year. It is often associated with ideas of karma, justice, and tying up loose ends. It is a time of reflection and appreciation for the year soon to end.

As always, emphasize those aspects of the festival that speak to you. It is most important that the ceremony have meaning for those taking part in it, so stress those themes that will have the greatest relevance to those present.

. . . .

Air

For this ritual we will cleanse the space with mineral salts and alcohol. To do this you will need some mineral salts of the sort used for making bath salts. These should be readily available in a craft store. Epsom salts also work well. You will also need rubbing alcohol. It is best to use the mineral salts in their natural state. You can sometimes successfully use bath salts, depending on how they have been made, but they will not be as effective.

Have everyone already assembled.

Place the mineral salts in a fire-resistant container. A tinfoil container, such as those used for baking, is ideal since the mineral salts will leave a residue that is hard to clean. Add alcohol to the mineral salts, enough to soak them well.

Now say something like:

"Behold, we shall join together to cleanse this space. Even as these salts burn, so too shall all negative energy in this space be transformed and transmuted, consecrated and blessed. So too shall our own energy be cleansed and blessed as well. So mote it be!"

All: *"So mote it be!"*

Now light the mineral salts using a match, candle, or consecrated lighter. They will set up a bright, pale, cleansing flame that will raise the vibration of the energy.

Allow the mineral salts to burn for a bit, and then lead the people in a visualization to internalize the effects. You might do it like this:

"Behold the flame, dancing before us. Feel the strength in it, the power. Feel its energy, moving and transforming all it touches, transmuting all negativity. Imagine the flame growing brighter, expanding, growing larger and larger. See the flame expand to fill the space between us, then expand beyond us. See it grow and expand farther and farther, until it fills our entire ritual space with transformative light. Feel the energy moving all around you, feel the energy moving within you as

*well. Feel it raising your vibration,
cleansing you, eliminating all
negative energy. Even as the fire
burns, the vibration rises. Negative
energy is transformed and becomes
positive. The circle is cleansed,
and we are cleansed with it."*

Allow the fire to burn until it goes out.
Then say something like:

"Behold, it is done. So mote it be!"

All: *"So mote it be!"*

We will now cast the circle. For this ritual we will use a spiral casting. Have the people assemble at the east and wait until the ritual space is cleansed. Then lead them in, single file: process deosil in a circle around the edges of the ritual space, marking out the circle of art. As you do this, visualize a trail of white light being created behind you. As you come around to the east again, this trail of white light will form a circle. Process around the circle three times, imagining the white light becoming clearer and brighter as you go. As you do this you might want to chant. A good chant might be:

*"The spiral is a circle that
continues past its start*

*Ever rising, weaving, winding!
With the magic of the heart!*

*We spiral round our temple
make it holy, make it ours!*

*And our dancing forms a circle
as mighty as the stars!*

*The spiral is a circle that
continues past its start*

*Ever rising, weaving, winding!
With the magic of the heart!*

*We are one within our circle
with the God and the Goddess*

*Who move through us in the
circle as our circle we now bless!*

*The spiral is a circle that
continues past its start*

*Ever rising, weaving, winding!
With the magic of the heart!"*

After the third time around, stop and lead the people in a visualization to formalize the circle. You might do it like this:

*"Behold, with our steps we have
cast a circle, created a place
between the world of humankind*

185

and of the Mighty Ones. Imagine it around us. See it as a wall of light surrounding us. Bright, shining white light. Imagine it clearly, strongly, a circle of art to focus and to contain the powers we shall raise herein. Around, around, around, about! All good stay in and all ill keep out!"

Now invoke the quarters.

. . . .

Fire

In this ritual we will invoke the quarters through the forms of the God. This can be particularly good for the Lesser (solar) Sabbats or other rituals that honor the masculine polarity.

Begin in the east. Use a wand, sacred tool of fire, or if you prefer, use your fingers. Raise the wand, imagining as you do so a column of pure white light arising in the east, at the border of the circle. See the column as strong and pure and filled with energy. Say something like:

East

"I invoke you, O God, in your form as Golden Lord of the East, Hero and Champion of the Goddess, Lord of the Dawn and of Spring! Your breath is in the air and the greening buds of leaves and flowers. May your wind bring fresh ideas and inspiration to our circle!"

Now move to the next quarter. Again raise the wand and imagine a column of pure white light arising in the quarter. Say something like:

South

"I invoke you, O God, in your form as Red Lord of the South, Lover and Consort of the Goddess, Lord of Noonday and of Summer! Your spirit is in the fire and the growing crops of the fields. May your flames bring passion and vitality to our circle!"

Now move to the next quarter. Again raise the wand and imagine a column of pure white light arising in the quarter. Say something like:

West

"I invoke you, O God, in your form as Blue Lord of the West, King and Right Hand of the Goddess, Lord of Sunset and of Autumn! Your blood is in the water, in the harvest that is reaped, and in the falling leaves.

*May your waves bring empathy
and compassion to our circle!"*

Now move to the next quarter. Again raise the wand and imagine a column of pure white light arising in the quarter. Say something like:

North

*"I invoke you, O God, in your
form as Green Lord of the North,
Sorcerer and Guardian for the
Goddess of the Gates of Life
and Death, Lord of Midnight
and of Winter! Your flesh is
in the earth, the frosted trees
and seeds that wait for rebirth.
May your soil bring wisdom and
understanding to our circle!"*

Now it is time to invoke Deity. Since the Lesser Sabbats are solar ceremonies, the God will be invoked first. In this case we shall invoke the God not in any particular personal form, but in his archetype as King! You will remember from First Degree studies that some personal forms of this archetype include Jupiter, Ra, and Nodens.

The priest raises his arms to call upon the God. He might say something like:

Priest: *"O God, we do invoke you in
your form as King! Lord of the Wheel*

*of Karma! You turn the Wheel of the
Goddess upon which the threads of
Fate are spun, so that actions return
upon themselves and divine balance is
maintained. Lord of the Harvest, you
sacrifice yourself that life may endure
through winter—illustrating the karmic interdependence of life upon life.
Join us O God, we pray, in this sacred
festival! We bid you hail and welcome!"*

All: *"Hail and welcome!"*

Now imagine the God entering the circle. Imagine it in any way that makes sense to you, perhaps by imagining the God in human form, as a shower of glittering light, or as a ball or tower of light appearing in the circle.

Now let us invoke the Goddess in her archetype as Mother: in this sense, as the ruling Mother of the harvest. You will remember from First Degree studies that some personal forms of this archetype include Isis, Yemaya, and Mati Suira-Zemlya.

The priestess raises her arms to call upon the Goddess. She might say something like:

Priestess: *"O Goddess, we do invoke you in
your form of Harvest Mother. All-bountiful and Provident One, you sustain*

Mabon

187

your children through the winter with the food of the earth, your body. It is you who decree the fall of the crops, you who decree the death of the God, you who weave the threads of karma from which the web of life is fashioned. All things depend upon all others—and all proceed from you. Join us we pray, O Goddess, in this our holy rite! We bid you hail and welcome!"

All: *"Hail and welcome!"*

Now visualize the Goddess entering the circle.

Finally, invoke the ancestors. You might say something like:

> *"O mighty ancestors, beloved ones who have gone before, we invoke you and ask you to join us and to bless us! Ancestors of the Correllian Tradition, priestesses and priests, mothers and uncles of the lineage, spiritual family that aids and supports us, lend us your inspiration and your love, your guidance and your aid this night, we pray. Beloved ones, we bid you hail and welcome!"*

All: *"Hail and welcome!"*

. . . .
Spirit

Begin by discussing the nature of the Mabon festival. Like all Sabbats, Mabon has many aspects you can talk about, depending upon where you wish to put your emphasis. In discussing the nature of Mabon you might say something like:

> *"Mabon is the feast of the autumn equinox. Now are night and day again equal, and perfect balance reigns. The God is waning, days grow shorter, the crops are falling as the harvests progress. But even as his power wanes, he comes into his own as King and Counselor. Karma, the Divine Plan, and justice are emphasized. We will eat through the winter because the crops have died for us; all things are connected and affect each other. The death of one is life to another. All is in balance and all things are as they should be. Let us then focus upon balance, and seek that balance in our lives."*

. . . .
Act of Power
Chakra Balancing

Our first act of power for Mabon is a chakra-balancing meditation. This draws its inspiration from the equal hours of day and night at equinox. This meditation is also very appropriate for Ostara, and for that matter can be used at any other time when there is a need to bring energies into balance.

You might lead the meditation something like this:

"Let us begin by clearing and releasing all excess energy. Let all excess energy pour out of you. Let any tension, stress, or anxiety pour out of you like water, running down your body and out through your feet into the earth, where it may be reused for better purposes.

Now let us become aware of our heart chakra. Imagine it as a ball of clear white light glowing in the center of your chest. See the light as clear, strong, and bright, and if it is mottled or occluded in any way, take a moment to clear it. Imagine the heart chakra like a sun inside your chest, glowing with light and energy and strength.

Now from your heart chakra, send down a beam of light into the earth. See the beam of light

going down through your body, through your legs, through your feet, and into the earth, down into the soil, deeper and deeper, into the rich earth, down into the rock, deep into the bedrock, further and further through the rocky mantle of the earth, until at last it enters the molten center of the earth.

Send your beam of light into the glowing magma, the warm and pulsing heart of Mother Earth. Feel the heat of it, feel the strength of it, feel the energy of the earth, glowing hot and golden. It is full of love and peace, strength and power.

Now feel the golden energy of the earth moving up through your beam of light. Feel the strong energy of the earth moving up through the bedrock, moving up through the soil, up through your feet, and into your body. Let the golden energy come up through your legs and into your torso to fill your heart chakra. Let the hot and glowing energy of the earth fill your heart chakra. Feel the warmth and strength and peace

Mabon

189

of the earth filling your heart, feel her burning love and joy. Let it fill your heart chakra, then move out through your whole body, out into your shoulders and your abdomen, into your arms and your legs, all the way out to your fingers and toes, until you are filled completely with the golden light of the earth.

Savor the energy. Feel it flow through you, filling and suffusing you. Imagine the golden energy moving out from the edges of your physical body now, beginning to fill your aura. See the golden energy filling your aura, expanding and moving around you until you are surrounded by a ball of golden energy, until you and your aura are completely filled by the energy of the earth.

Now become aware of your heart chakra again. As the strong and loving energy of the earth fills you and moves within you, send out another beam of light from your heart chakra. Imagine this beam of light moving upward, up through your head, up into the air, out into the sky. Feel the beam of light going up farther and farther, higher and higher. Feel the beam of light moving up into the clouds, then past them into the upper reaches of the atmosphere.

Feel the energy of the heavens, airy and broadly expansive. Where Earth is hot and passionate, filled with warm emotion, the heavens are cool and analytical, free-floating and mercurial. The energy of the heavens is clear and precise, glittering with a silvery blue-white light.

Now imagine the energy of the heavens begins to move down your beam of light. Cool and glittering, it moves down through the beam of light, down from the outer atmosphere into the clouds, down through the clouds into the sky, down, down, moving down the beam, down farther until it enters through the top of your head, moving down through your neck and into your chest to fill your heart chakra.

Feel the cool, sharp energy of the heavens fill your heart chakra. Feel its clarity and precision. Let it fill your heart chakra, then move out through your whole body, out into your shoulders and your abdomen, into your arms and your legs, all the way out to your fingers and toes, until you are filled completely with the silvery light of the heavens.

And now let the warm, loving energy of the earth and the cool, determined energy of the heavens come into balance within you. Feel the two energies balancing one another, bringing your own energy and all of your chakras into balance as they do so. Feel the movement of the energy within you as they come into perfect balance and harmony.

On this night of equinox, the Divine Mother Goddess and Divine Father God are in perfect harmony and balance. Let us too be in perfect balance. Mother Goddess and Father God, bless us we pray with the love you share between yourselves and with all

things. May we, too, love as you, and may our lives be ever sweet."

You might follow this with a chant and perhaps a dance. A good chant might be:

"Blessed be the Mother Earth
Blessed be the Father Sky
Blessed be their union within me!
Blessed be the Mother Earth
Blessed be the Father Sky
Blessed be them in eternity!
Blessed be the Mother Earth
Blessed be the Father Sky
Blessed be their Divine Harmony!"

Now clear and release the excess energy from the meditation before going on with the rest of your ritual.

• • • •

Water

For our toast in this ritual you will need two people to represent the Goddess and God. You will also need two beverages. The person representing the Goddess should have a dark beverage such as a red grape juice. The person representing the God should have a light beverage such as a white grape juice. The chalice will be held between them.

The Goddess should go first. Let the person representing the Goddess raise up the dark beverage and say something like:

Mabon

"In the beginning was the Goddess. And she was alone and without form in the void of chaos before the first creation. But she longed to create, to work her will and give form to existence. And the Goddess dreamed and the Goddess planned, and the Goddess longed and from her longing came the first creation.

In the name of the Goddess may the blessing be upon this juice!"

Let the person representing the Goddess now bless the dark juice, filling it with light and energy.

Now let the person representing the God hold up the light beverage and say something like:

"And from the Goddess was created the God. The Goddess divided herself, sending all of the fiery, active, physical aspects of herself into the God and retaining all of the watery, malleable, spiritual aspects for herself. And the God exploded out from the Goddess in the explosion of the first creation, sending fire and light in all directions.

In the name of the God may the blessing be upon this juice!"

Now let the person representing the God bless the light juice, filling it with energy and light.

Then the person representing the Goddess continues:

"In time, the light of the God cooled and took form, becoming suns and planets and asteroids. The universe took shape and the Goddess was pleased. She desired to be part of this universe, to rejoin with the God and be one with him. But he fled from her as the mouse flees before the cat."

Now the person representing the God:

"And she took counsel of her Highest Self, which told her that 'To rise you must fall.' And so the Goddess created the many souls and sent them into matter, so that through them she could unite with the God. And so was the world we know created."

Now let them fill the chalice together, so that the dark juice and the light juice are mingled.

Now pronounce a final blessing upon the chalice:

"In the name of the Goddess and of the God may this chalice be blessed, that it may be a token of the bond of love that exists between ourselves and them, and between them and all of creation!"

Let the person representing the Goddess draw up energy from the earth to bless the chalice in the name of the Goddess. Simultaneously, may the person representing the God draw down energy from the heavens to bless the chalice in the name of the God. As they meet in the middle, finish the blessing:

"So mote it be!"

All: *"So mote it be!"*

Now pass the chalice deosil around the circle, letting each person drink in their turn. You should go last and offer the final bit to Spirit.

Or if you prefer, you can pass out paper cups and fill them from the chalice, asking everyone to wait and drink at the same time. Make sure to have a cup for Spirit. If you do it this way, you may wish to offer a toast such as:

"To the Goddess! To the God! To us!"

All: *"To the Goddess! To the God! To us!"*

. . . .

Earth

Now you will close the ceremony and open the circle.

Begin by giving thanks to the ancestors and the deities.

"Beloved ancestors, you who have gone before, your wisdom and your example guide us. We pray that you will be with us and aid us as we go forward, that we may call upon the strength and knowledge of the past, even as we build the future. We thank you for your presence and your aid this night and at all times. May you blessed be in all things. We offer you our love and our respect! We bid you hail and farewell!"

All: *"Hail and farewell!"*

Priest: *"O holy Harvest King! Lord of Justice, Protector and Provider for Your Children! We thank you for your presence and your aid this night, and at all*

Mabon

times. *We offer you our love and our respect! We bid you hail and farewell!"*

All: *"Hail and farewell!"*

Priestess: *"All-bountiful and Provident Mother Goddess, Weaver of the Web of the Universe. We thank you for your presence and your aid this night and at all times. We offer you our love and our respect! We bid you hail and farewell!"*

All: *"Hail and farewell!"*

Now thank each quarter. Start in the north.

North

"We thank you, O God, in your form as Green Lord of the North, Sorcerer and Lord of Midnight and of Winter! We are grateful for your guidance and your aid in this our holy ritual! From our hearts, with love and with respect, we bid you hail and farewell!"

All: *"Hail and farewell!"*

Using the wand, pull down the tower of white light that was erected when the north was called.

Now turn to the west.

West

"We thank you, O God, in your form as Blue Lord of the West, King and Lord of Sunset and of Autumn! We are grateful for your guidance and your aid in this our holy ritual! From our hearts, with love and with respect, we bid you hail and farewell!"

All: *"Hail and farewell!"*

Using the wand, pull down the tower of white light that was erected when the west was called.

Now turn to the south.

South

"We thank you, O God, in your form as Red Lord of the South, Lover and Lord of Noonday and of Summer! We are grateful for your guidance and your aid in this our holy ritual! From our hearts, with love and with respect, we bid you hail and farewell!"

All: *"Hail and farewell!"*

Using the wand, pull down the tower of white light that was erected when the south was called.

Now turn to the east.

East

"We thank you, O God, in your form as Golden Lord of the East, Hero and Lord of the Dawn and of Spring! We are grateful for your guidance and your aid in this our holy ritual! From our hearts, with love and with respect, we bid you hail and farewell!"

All: *"Hail and farewell!"*

Using the wand, pull down the tower of white light that was erected when the east was called.

Now you must open the circle. Begin in the east. Take up the athame and point it toward the eastern quarter. Devoke the circle, walking tuathail around it, imagining the barrier of light disappearing and returning back into the tip of the athame. Now speak the charm:

"Behold: As above, so below! As the universe, so the soul! As within, so without! May the circle be open but never broken! Merry meet, merry part, and merry meet again!"

Now have everyone cleanse and release all excess energy.

Act of Power #2
Prayer Ties

We have already discussed that the Mabon festival deals with issues of balance. One aspect of balance is that of justice and karma. This is a holiday that deals with the idea of reaping what you sow, and it is a theme that is well to hit on. The idea of karma and the Threefold Law is that what you do comes back to you—not just once but many times until you learn the lesson of the actions and thus no longer form an attachment to the pattern.

The undeveloped person thinks of karma primarily in terms of its effects on other people, as a kind of divine "Don't worry, they'll get theirs" sort of thing. But wise people think of karma in terms of its effects on themselves. We must always be mindful of the karmic effect of our actions and consider how we shall feel on the receiving end.

Our second act of power deals with just these issues. This act of power is a variation on the technique of using prayer ties that is found in our Second Degree spell for Lesson IV under the heading "Magical Automatons."

For this act of power you will need several lengths of ribbon. The ribbon may be of any kind, and there should be at least one for each person present. You will also need a tree. The tree must be a real tree,

Mabon

195

which means this act of power should be used either with an outdoor ritual, or it must be completed after the circle is opened by proceeding outside to the designated tree. Another variation might be to have a potted tree that is indoors for the ritual, then subsequently taken outside.

You might choose to offer several different colors of ribbon, from which people can choose the one they feel is most appropriate for them, or you can choose to have them all be the same color. The ribbon may be either short or long but should not be too long.

Ask everyone to think of an action they regret—a person to whom they have done wrong or a situation in which they acted badly. We all have things that we regret: times when we said or did things we shouldn't have, or when we didn't say or do things that we should have. It is part of being human. These regrets form blockages, karmic attachments. Have each person think of one such situation; we are going to pray for healing for that situation.

Pass out the ribbon. Everyone should take one.

Ask everyone to think about the situation they wish to do healing for, and what it is they regret doing or not doing. Examine the emotions. Who was hurt by this? What part was your responsibility? What needs to be healed? Imagine the situation clearly and have it strongly in your mind.

Ask everyone to hold their ribbon in their hand. Have them imagine the ribbon filled with energy, radiating white light. Instruct them to concentrate strongly upon the situation to be healed. Imagine the situation strongly and focus sending healing energy to it. Imagine the situation and everyone in it while you charge the ribbon for their healing.

Now offer a prayer, something like this:

"Divine Mother Goddess, Divine Father God, help us, we pray, to heal these things that we think of now! Lend your strength to ours, that these things may be healed. Take the healing energy we offer and send it to where it is most needed in these situations, with harm toward none and in accordance with the free will of all. As we tie our prayers into the branches of this holy and venerable tree, we pray that our prayers shall be carried upon the wind, swift as thoughts and certain as rivers. May they be carried forward into manifestation as surely as the wind blows. As the flower gives rise to the fruit, and the fruit gives rise to the seed, so may this healing

take effect. Behold, by our will and with your aid. So mote it be!"

If you are outside or using a potted tree (either of which should be included inside the circle for this act of power), immediately tie your ribbons to the tree's branches. If you prefer, other types of ornaments besides ribbons may be used, but they must be biodegradable. Offer another prayer now:

"Holy Tree, you, too, are a perfect manifestation of the Goddess. We pray that as our spell is released into being you will aid and guide it with your strength, born of the earth. Even as the wind blows through your boughs, may this healing take effect, carried forward by the divine elements. So mote it be!"

If you must wait until the end of the ritual to proceed out to your tree, then place the charged ribbons upon the altar after the first prayer. When you have had your after-ritual procession and placed your ribbons on the tree, then offer the second prayer.

· · · ·
Act of Power #3
Labyrinth

Our final act of power for Mabon is the labyrinth.

The labyrinth is appropriate for Mabon because it deals with issues of inner examination, which connect to the Sabbat's ideas of balance and justice. Also, the labyrinth's complex shape is suggestive of the effects of karma, radiating out from a central action in branching paths that can be hard to retrace.

The most famous labyrinth is the great Labyrinth of Minos from ancient Greek myth. Pasiphae, wife of the Cretan king Minos, gave birth to a child who was half bull and half man, the Minotaur. Minos employed the greatest architect of the time, Daedalus, to build a labyrinth to contain the Minotaur. Each year, seven youths and seven maidens would be sent into the labyrinth, never to return. Eventually Theseus defeated the Minotaur with the help of the Cretan Princess Ariadne.

It is generally thought that this myth represents a Greek treatment of actual Cretan religion, albeit in a very misunderstood form. It has been learned that the bull was a very important element in Cretan religion, representing the God in his forms as King and Sorcerer. Minos appears to have been an actual figure in Cretan myth, and his role in Greek myth as an

Mabon

ideal of just kingship and as Judge of the Dead presumably reflects how the Cretans viewed him. Presumably the Bull is Minos' avatar, and the Minotaur represents this.

Minos' role as Old God and as King/Judge connects strongly to the themes of Mabon.

Of course, as you will see, the labyrinth is equally appropriate for other Sabbats as well, being an excellent technique for inner workings, and you should not feel that its use is only recommended for Mabon.

How on Earth does one make a labyrinth for a ritual? Well, there are several ways, and it's not as hard as you might expect.

A labyrinth is basically a maze-like route to a small, open center space. The maze can be very complex, but it can also be fairly simple. In its simplest form, a labyrinth can be merely a spiral leading into a center.

One of the most beautiful ways to erect a labyrinth for a ritual is to mark out the path in candles. The effect of this is extremely memorable. In creating a candle labyrinth, you must be careful to minimize the risk of fire with sweeping robes and candles. This can be a serious consideration. It is important to make sure the path is wide enough so that people can pass without knocking over the candles. How the candles are set up is important, too. Do not just use open candles. Jar candles are a good possibility, and I have seen them used

to great effect. Candelaria are a good idea as well. Candelaria are votive candles set into a specially constructed holder that in essence forms a small lantern. The holder can be made from a rolled-down paper bag, with the candle set in the middle well away from the walls, or from a cut-down plastic milk carton.

Another dramatic way to create a labyrinth is to paint it onto canvas, using ordinary house paint. This has the advantage of being permanent and portable. Kits are available to re-create the famous labyrinth of Chartres in this manner. However, it is not necessary to use a kit, as you can design and create your own labyrinth on canvas in this manner.

Both of these techniques require a certain amount of money for the purchase of candles or of paint and canvas. But it is also possible to do a labyrinth in a way that does not require any outward physical form. To do this, you blindfold everyone, have them join hands, and lead them in a spiral or other more complex path to the center space.

Ideally, the center space should be large enough to hold several people at once, as this allows group activity in the center of the labyrinth, which can be very good. But it is important that the act of entering and leaving the labyrinth not be too quick, as there is a technique to using the labyrinth. It's not just a matter of walking or dancing

Chapter
XI

198

through the maze. It is a walking meditation. The labyrinth is an externalization of the mental/spiritual process that the people are passing through.

One way to do this is to have everyone choose a goal to manifest. As they walk into the labyrinth, have them focus on creating their goal. At the center they should offer a prayer or incantation for their goal. And as they walk out of the labyrinth, they should concentrate on receiving the goal and imagine what it will be like for the goal to have come to pass.

This can also be done with a question. As the people walk into the labyrinth, they focus on their question. In the center of the labyrinth, they formally state their question with a prayer or incantation and open themselves to an answer. As they walk out of the labyrinth, they focus on the knowledge that the answer is on its way to them.

Another way to do a labyrinth is to have people focus on the idea of going inside themselves as they walk into the labyrinth. At the center of the labyrinth an act of power is performed. Then as they walk out of the labyrinth, people focus on returning to the everyday world. The act of power at the center of the labyrinth may be any number of things. You can have everyone meditate, opening themselves to whatever Spirit may have to tell them. You may have a bowl of divinatory tokens, each person taking one and meditating on it. Or you might have everyone do a group meditation, such as the chakra-balancing meditation given above or any other group meditation. Do whatever you think will be best and most effective for the group at this time.

Depending upon exactly how you are doing your labyrinth, you may wish to enliven it with a steady drumbeat or with chants as people enter and leave the labyrinth. But if you are focusing on meditation, be careful not to break the meditative atmosphere with disruptive music. You might also try dancing the labyrinth, depending upon the temperament and athleticism of your group.

Although a labyrinth can be a lot of work to create, it is also impressive and memorable and can be a very effective ritual technique.

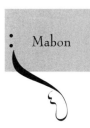

Mabon

I hope that you have enjoyed this discussion of ritual in theory and practice, and that it helps you in your personal vocation. As you go forward, I think you will find that creating and organizing group ritual will be not merely one of the practical functions of your vocation but also one of its great joys.

When we do solitary ritual we derive many benefits: we grow closer to Deity and to our own Higher Self; we grow spiritually and transform our lives for the better; and we experience for ourselves the nature and existence of the soul and of the Spirit world. Yet when we do group ritual we are helping others to achieve these same results, and there is a pleasure to be found in helping others and watching their growth unfold that is different from the pleasure we derive from our own growth. To know that you have made a positive difference in another person's life is one of the greatest rewards spirituality has to offer.

When I look back on many years of group ritual, it is not for the most part

Conclusion

what I myself did or felt that I remember, but rather the reactions of others: the joy shared in communal worship, especially by those who had previously thought they were alone; the occasional surprise at the strength of energy, especially by those who had never felt it before; the elation of direct spiritual experience, especially for those who had doubted the real existence of Deity and the soul; and the unfolding of spiritual growth on the part of so many good people who just needed the support of others like themselves and a little guidance to help them along the way. That is the real point of groups and group ritual—what it does for people. You will find that this is the greatest joy.

I was taught that we are not given spiritual knowledge and understanding so that they can be hidden and hoarded. We are given these things as tools not only to help ourselves but also to help other people and the world as a whole—to make it a better world than we ourselves found it. After all, we will be back this way again, and again.

I hope that you have found these ideas on ritual theory and practice to be a useful tool, in building your own better world.

Blessings to you,

Rev. Don